T0346761

BUFFALO BILL AND THE BIRTH OF AMERICAN CELEBRITY

KELLEN CUTSFORTH

TWODOT®

GUILFORD, CONNECTICUT
HELENA, MONTANA

A · TWODOT® · BOOK

An imprint of The Rowman & Littlefield Publishing Group, Inc.
4501 Forbes Blvd., Ste. 200
Lanham, MD 20706
www.rowman.com

Distributed by NATIONAL BOOK NETWORK

Copyright © 2021 Kellen Cutsforth

All photos courtesy of the Denver Public Library unless otherwise noted

All rights reserved. No part of this book may be reproduced in any form or by any electronic or mechanical means, including information storage and retrieval systems, without written permission from the publisher, except by a reviewer who may quote passages in a review.

British Library Cataloguing in Publication Information available

Library of Congress Cataloging-in-Publication Data

Names: Cutsforth, Kellen, author.
Title: Buffalo Bill and the birth of American celebrity / Kellen Cutsforth.
Description: Guilford, Connecticut : TwoDot, An imprint of The Rowman &
    Littlefield Publishing Group, Inc., [2021] | Includes bibliographical
    references and index. | Summary: "The story of Buffalo Bill's Wild West
    show and of a visionary whose real-life experiences, and embellishments,
    created an entertainment phenomenon that became a worldwide sensation"—
    Provided by publisher.
Identifiers: LCCN 2020043908 (print) | LCCN 2020043909 (ebook) | ISBN
    9781493047420 (hardback) | ISBN 9781493047437 (epub)
Subjects: LCSH: Buffalo Bill's Wild West Show—History. | Buffalo Bill,
    1846-1917. | Buffalo Bill's Combination (Theater troupe)—History. |
    Wild west shows—United States—History. | Curiosities and wonders—West
    (U.S.)—History. | West (U.S.)—History. | Entertainers—West
    (U.S.)—Biography.
Classification: LCC GV1821.B8 C87 202 (print) | LCC GV1821.B8 (ebook) |
    DDC 978/.02092 [B]—dc23
LC record available at https://lccn.loc.gov/2020043908
LC ebook record available at https://lccn.loc.gov/2020043909

♾™ The paper used in this publication meets the minimum requirements of American National Standard for Information Sciences—Permanence of Paper for Printed Library Materials, ANSI/NISO Z39.48-1992.

CONTENTS

Foreword v

Introduction vii

CHAPTER 1: Every Idea Is Inspired 1

CHAPTER 2: Experiences Make the Man 17

CHAPTER 3: From Prairie to Playhouse 31

CHAPTER 4: The Launch of a Legend and the Loss of a Friend 43

CHAPTER 5: Superman before Superman 53

CHAPTER 6: An Unlikely Cast of Characters 73

CHAPTER 7: Unstable Ground 87

CHAPTER 8: Hail to the King! 103

CHAPTER 9: "Heroes Get Remembered but Legends Never Die" . . . 127

Notes 143

Bibliography 163

Index 171

About the Author 176

FOREWORD

This is the West, sir. When the legend becomes fact, print the legend." Those immortal lines from John Ford's classic Western film *The Man Who Shot Liberty Valence* sum up our mythology of the American West to elegant perfection. The mythology of the Western, fact and fiction, is a cross-pollination in our grand consciousness of history, movies, and literature. Our uniquely American myth strikes a universal chord in people the world over.

Historically, the first real-life American individual to exploit and embody the western legend and mythos to popular fame was Buffalo Bill Cody, the subject of this book. Cody reinvented himself through reality and imagination as a bigger-than-life figure to the general public, and author Kellen Cutsforth makes a good case that the popularity of the Western in popular culture as we know it originated with Cody.

With his Buffalo Bill's Wild West traveling show, Cody brought historical western figures like gunfighter Wild Bill Hickok and Indian chief Sitting Bull to his live stage, creating the first show business dramatizations of the Old West for audiences, using actual people and re-creating true events in his show to give the public a taste of the true West. Chock-full of colorful tales and anecdotes involving the real-life personages and events, from young sharpshooter Annie Oakley's touching friendship with Sitting Bull to a command performance before Queen Victoria in England that became a triumph of US and British diplomacy, the book never fails to hold our interest.

Drawing relevant parallels to modern celebrity and branding, the promotional techniques Buffalo Bill Cody used to create his image and fame will be instantly recognizable to anybody familiar with social media or online promotion today, showing that in terms of celebrity culture, what's new is old.

In this tight, informative book loaded with factual detail, Kellen Cutsforth gives us a fascinating summary of a major figure in the American West, whose influence on the Western genre continues to this day.

—Eric Red, director and screenwriter

INTRODUCTION

Imagine someone asked you, "Close your eyes and think of the Old West. Now tell me what you see?" What images would you conjure up? Would you see desperadoes robbing a stagecoach? Little Annie Oakley making incredible trick shots? Perhaps you envision Indians in full war regalia attacking a farmhouse? Or maybe you perceive these great people in a more noble light, as they deliver swift justice to General George Armstrong Custer and his band of bluecoats on a blood-soaked prairie during the scorching summer of 1876? Do you see the Pony Express? Perhaps you visualize mountain men and majestic buffalo? Gunfighters and cowboys? Pioneers circling their wagons to fend off an attack, or awe-inspiring Indian war dances? If these are any of the pictures you see running through your mind's eye, then you have subconsciously been influenced by Buffalo Bill's Wild West without even realizing it.

In 1883, William Frederick "Buffalo Bill" Cody created the entertainment spectacle known as Buffalo Bill's Wild West. The outdoor show was filled with authentic cowboys, Indians, and animals that at one time populated the American West. Since its initial debut, the immense popularity of the enterprise, and the ardent fan following it achieved, has been woven into the very fabric of our society. It truly remains at the forefront of our national consciousness. Buffalo Bill's Wild West and the exhibitions and ideals it portrayed also remain ingrained in the minds of millions of people all over the world.

William Frederick Cody can be seen as America's first celebrity and is the inventor of our national idea of the Wild West. By incorporating his real-life experiences along with embellishments and use of pioneering promotional techniques, Cody was able to brand his nickname, "Buffalo Bill," and make it a household term.

Bill's sustained popularity is evidenced by the numerous institutions, peppered all over the country, that continue to celebrate his legacy. Reenactors portray the showman at numerous venues, from rodeos to concerts to modern Wild West show performances. Thousands of books, pieces of music, and movies featuring Cody as a character have been produced over the decades. Everyone from adults to children continue to celebrate his memory in one form or another.

This book is not intended to be a biography of Cody, which has been done ad nauseam. Nor is it intended to be an academic treatise detailing the good or ills committed by Buffalo Bill or the participants of the Wild West show. Instead, this book is an examination and celebration of the making of Buffalo Bill and his most famous Wild West show. This volume will look at the influences, relationships, and moments that led Cody to create his most well-loved and well-remembered enterprise.

CHAPTER 1
Every Idea Is Inspired

A blisteringly hot ball of fire hangs high over the prairie as a lone rider clad in full-fringed buckskins sits tall in the saddle. He is motionless, perched on the back of a well-muscled stallion whose lathered white coat glistens in the midday sun like fine bone china. Raising a beaded-gloved hand to his brow, the scout shields his eyes as he surveys the sun-drenched plains. The old pathfinder then draws back his long silvery locks and cups his ear, piquing it to attention.

Growing in volume, echoes of Indian war whoops and the steady monotone beat of drums rise like a coming tide over the sagebrush-peppered prairie. Like a well-rehearsed signal, the old scout raises his hand high above his Stetson-covered head. In an instant, a multitude of cavalry officers ride up around the lone sentry, followed by a column of blue-coated soldiers marching in step with the beat of their own drum and bugle corps.

Indians, now visible, swarm like a hive of angry bees bent on destruction. Bright and colorful war paint is slathered on their bodies, accentuating eagle feather war-bonnets affixed to their heads. Horses stamp and whinny in anticipation of the coming battle. The mounted braves are an impressive sight. These young men represent the heart of the Sioux nation. They stand in the gap for their people as they prepare to fend off the massive military invasion force. Their whoops and undulating gestures let forth a collective primal scream that exclaims, "We will not go quietly without a fight!"

Buffalo Bill sitting on his horse "Charlie"

Suddenly, a gunshot rings out! The silence that washes over the field of combatants is palpable. Acrid smoke from a freshly fired rifle round wafts in the air. No one dares move. Suddenly, as if on cue, a young brave wobbles then falls from his horse to the sun-scorched earth in a plume of dust. Like a starter's pistol signaling the beginning of a race, the fight is on! Both sides ride headlong into war as arrows zip and bullets fly. Chaos reigns!

The aged scout proves his mettle by riding to the front of the column and waving his Stetson high around his head like a lariat. He urges his fellow soldiers forward while bellowing out a war whoop of his own. The scout's pearl-white stallion rears on its hind legs before tearing into a gallop. Soldiers advance close behind. Man and beast thrust forward into the fray, meeting their hard-charging adversaries headlong. Arrows and bullets fired in the old scout's direction find no purchase. The old vanguard cuts a swath through the Indians without incurring so much as a scratch to either himself or his horseflesh. Employing the lever action on his Winchester rifle, the old man guns down braves right and left with repeated swiftness.

Despite his best efforts, however, his blue-coated brethren continue to fall all around him. The scout now seems to be the only one standing in the way of the entire battalion's utter annihilation. Unbelievably, he never runs low on cartridges or stamina. Then, as if preordained, reinforcements arrive from behind and cannons roar. When the smoke clears, everyone on the field of battle lies dead or dying save for the scout and one solitary brave whose feathered headdress is the length of a bride's wedding train. The two meet in the exact middle of the prairie and engage in pitched hand-to-hand combat. The scout eventually fells his foe with a single blow and takes the scalp of his slain enemy, raising it high to the heavens!

Enthralled by what they have witnessed, the surrounding stadium crowd rises to its collective feet! Stomping on the planks of a rickety wooden grandstand, the people cheer in one voice as they clap their hands wildly in approval. The old scout, better known as Buffalo Bill Cody, takes off his hat once more and salutes the vociferous onlookers. The adulation that follows is resounding. People applaud and hail this great scout of the prairie. Bill mounts his steed and rides out of the arena to the applause of the people. The actors, both Indians and soldiers, in this rehearsed and staged conflict rise to their feet and follow behind their fearless leader.

Exiting the arena, Buffalo Bill trots away from the adoring masses. Once he is out of view, he slowly slides from the saddle, his spurs hitting the earthen floor with a

Custer's charge reenactment for Buffalo Bill's Wild West, circa 1894

Native Americans dancing in Buffalo Bill's Wild West, 1901

clump. Bill's aging bones cannot take the pummeling of riding horses for hours on end like they used to. The aches and pains of age coupled with the heat of the day have the old scout sweating buckets and feeling exhausted. He flops down, coming to rest in a wooden chair that has been prepped for him backstage. One of the many actors he employs quietly brings him a brimming cup of cool, refreshing water that Cody's quaking hand nearly spills.

As Bill slakes his thirst, he peers through a peephole at the sharpshooters who are preparing to perform in front of the still-cheering arena crowd. He locks his gaze on the Little Sure Shot, Annie Oakley. Watching his most popular performer working on her quick-draw techniques, the old scout takes a second to reflect on her rise to fame, which is nearly intertwined with his own. Buffalo Bill's Wild West has made William Frederick "Buffalo Bill" Cody a household name and America's first true celebrity.

This enterprise has also allowed Bill to amass a great deal of personal wealth. Though he is the most recognized American in the world, Cody has not forgotten his days of riding for the Pony Express, hunting buffalo for the Kansas Pacific Railroad, and scouting for the military during the Plains Indian Wars. In fact, never missing an opportunity to promote, he has incorporated most of these events into his Wild West performances. While ruminating on this, Bill sits and reflects on the influences that helped him envision his enterprise.

Good ideas, like Buffalo Bill's Wild West, are rarely the product of one individual's own creative thoughts. In fact, most psychologists believe that everything one absorbs from the world around them is processed in one's brain and then various ideas spring forth from those thoughts. In many cases a product or concept already exists, and an individual gives his or her interpretation of that product or simply improves upon it.

In the case of Buffalo Bill's Wild West, the aspects of frontier life it embodied were nearly foreign concepts to the crowds who watched the circus-like spectacle. The show consisted of reenactments of historic battles combined with displays of showmanship, sharpshooting, buffalo hunts, horse racing, and rodeo-style events. Each show was three to four hours in length and began with a parade on horseback. The parade was a major ordeal—an affair that involved huge public crowds and multiple performers.[1] Not too entirely different from the parades currently held at Walt Disney's numerous theme parks every night.

Buffalo Bill's Wild West is considered the first outdoor Western show and is the first entertainment spectacle to incorporate promotional techniques like celebrity

Buffalo Bill watches at the peephole as his performers prepare to entertain the crowd in the arena, 1901.

endorsements, press kits, publicity stunts, op-ed articles, billboards, and product licensing.[2] Most of these techniques were introduced by Cody's publicist, "Arizona" John Burke.[3]

Buffalo Bill's Wild West was in many ways a unique venture, and pioneering in many entertainment aspects. However, it did have influences from endeavors preceding it. In fact, many of the first depictions of "western life" as a form of entertainment used the exhibition of American Indians. Early on, Indians were treated as museum displays. They were often exhibited as "oddities" or "attractions" and later as anthropological specimens.[4]

The native peoples of this country have long fascinated and inspired many who encountered them. When European and native cultures clashed beginning in the late fifteenth century, the disparities between these peoples were as obvious as night and day. These cultures' differing political and social structures, religious beliefs, and perceptions of wealth were completely at odds with each other.

When Spanish conquistador Hernán Cortés landed in current-day Veracruz, Mexico, on April 22, 1519, he embarked on a mission of subjugation and conversion of the Indians. This, unfortunately for Indians living in several regions of the country, was a scenario that repeated itself well into the late nineteenth century.

Though many confrontations between the two civilizations ended in bloodshed, some instigated by white settlers and some by Indians, not all the encounters between these peoples resulted in violence. Examples of concord between cultures took place all over the western United States. The Mormons in Utah Territory worked with the Southern Paiute tribes as early as 1854 to rebuild a one-hundred-foot-long conversion dam on the Santa Clara River.[5] And the interactions between Southern Cheyenne and Arapaho Indians with traders and mountain men along the Santa Fe Trail and specifically at Bent's Old Fort trading post from 1833 to 1849 are also great examples.[6]

There were commonalities among these peoples of differing races and beliefs, and in many cases there was a shared mutual respect. This is the stance that Buffalo Bill took regarding many of the native tribes, and how he incorporated them into his show. Bill was no doubt influenced by his own personal interactions with these people growing up, and that experience carried over to his business interactions with them. Unfortunately for many Indians, several of the showmen preceding Buffalo Bill treated them poorly and used them as oddities to be ogled by curious crowds.

Annie Oakley target shooting, 1892

Native American (Sioux) men and a white man and woman reenact an Indian attack on white settlers at their cabin in Buffalo Bill's Wild West, London, England. Photograph by E. Vandyk, circa 1892.

Though the native peoples of this land became main features in Buffalo Bill's Wild West, they were features in theatrical productions years before Cody employed them. As early as 1768, several Cherokee braves performed a war dance on the stage of New York's John Street Theatre.[7] In 1827, Iroquois warriors demonstrated a variety of battle techniques including a simulated scalping at Peale's Museum in Philadelphia.[8]

The artist George Catlin is credited with organizing the first western exposition in 1839 when he toured London, Brussels, and Paris with his paintings of Indians.[9] Catlin painted Indians for years and made portraits of more than forty-eight tribes before he decided to exhibit overseas. Under the title "Nature's Dignitaries," Catlin exhibited his art alongside local boys dressed as Indian braves adorned in warbonnets, whom he hired to whoop it up in front of royalty.[10]

After the success of these mock Indian shows, Catlin eventually hired several authentic Ojibwe Indians to re-create native dances, hunts, and scalpings. These Indians were showered with gifts by European audiences while they took photos with fans and signed autographs. Unfortunately for Catlin, all the hoopla surrounding his tour and art exhibition was not to last. He was saddled with expenses ranging from the cost of renting exhibition halls, traveling across Europe, paying for his performers and family, and hauling his art and artifacts all over the continent. When Catlin eventually returned to the United States, he was broke, and completely destitute.[11]

Not one to be outdone by these exploits, the biggest huckster and circus promoter of them all, P. T. Barnum, employed Indians in many of his shows and in the most exploitive way possible. In 1841 Barnum purchased Scudder's American Museum in New York City.[12] He quickly turned the institution into a combination zoo, museum, lecture hall, wax museum, theater, and freak show. Two years later in 1843, Barnum brought Sac, Fox, and Iowa Indians to New York and had them perform their native dances and participate in many warlike reenactments for audiences.[13]

Like many of the original "employers" of American Indians, Barnum had absolutely no experience with these people and therefore had a low opinion of them. In fact, Barnum, when corresponding with Moses Kimball of the Boston Museum, referenced the indigenous people by writing, "Damn Indians anyhow. They are a lazy, shiftless set of brutes but they will draw. The lazy devils want to be lying down nearly all the time, and as it looks so bad for them to be lying about the Museum, I have them stretched out in the workshop all day, some of them occasionally strolling about the Museum."[14]

Barnum held similar opinions about people of varying ethnicities and races. Later in life, however, he would have a change of heart toward black people, but he never showed much sympathy for American Indians. In fact, he continued to regard them as dirty, treacherous savages. When P. T. was not exhibiting Indian war dances, tomahawk battles, or other customs in the lecture hall of the American Museum, he often hired them out to compete in canoe races.[15]

Twenty years after he purchased the American Museum, Barnum brought some of the most powerful chiefs in the country to his museum, who happened to be in Washington, D.C., visiting Abraham Lincoln for a discussion on peace. Among the attending chiefs were Lone Wolf and White Bull of the Kiowa, and War Bonnet and Lean Bear of the Cheyenne. After convincing their interpreter to take them to New York to visit his museum, Barnum paraded the Indians around the city as often as he could and exhibited them regularly on the museum stage after he told them they were "honored guests."[16]

One of this group was apparently a notorious individual named Yellow Bear, who supposedly had killed numerous white people on the frontier. During the show, Barnum would make a great pretense of saying respectful and admiring things about him. Unfortunately for Yellow Bear, he could not understand what P. T. was really saying. Barnum would pat Yellow Bear on the shoulder and then introduce him as "the meanest black-hearted rascal that lives in the West," and as "a lying, thieving, treacherous, murderous monster." The chiefs eventually caught on to what Barnum was doing and angrily made their exit.[17]

P. T.'s use of native peoples in his exhibitions was often one of exploitation. He paid the Indians poorly, treated them as savage brutes and only used them to make a quick buck. In what was perhaps a deserving end for the business and indicative of his exploitive ways, in 1865 Barnum's American Museum burned to the ground. In what was described as "a horrific display," animals in the building jumped out of the windows only to be shot by police, and many of the animals who did not escape the blaze perished in their enclosures. It was reported that two large beluga whales, which clearly could not run, boiled to death in their tanks.[18]

As Barnum switched his sights from museum displays to traveling shows and circuses, he continued to incorporate Indians. In 1882 Barnum toured with a segment titled "Indian Life" and traveled with an "Indian Band."[19] Two years later Barnum debuted his Grand Ethnological Congress of Nations, in which he presented all

Col. Tim McCoy & His Indian Line Up, Ringling Brothers and Barnum & Bailey Combined Circus. *Photographer Edward J. Kelty, July 9, 1935.*

the known world's "uncivilized races" and "savage and barbarous tribes," including a group of North American Sioux, Zulus, Polynesians, and Australian Aborigines.[20]

Barnum did indeed employ Indians in his show forty years before William Frederick "Buffalo Bill" Cody envisioned his Wild West. Bill as a young man may have had exposure to Barnum's shows, which may have influenced him to employ American Indians in his enterprise as a good business practice. But the way the two men treated the native peoples was vastly at odds.

Buffalo Bill found inspiration for his show from many other sources than just the country's native peoples. Another contrast between Barnum and Bill was how each man perceived and envisioned his business. From the onset, Bill saw his Wild West as a historical reenactment. Unlike Barnum who made money from "suckers" to get rich as quickly as possible, Bill never used the term "show" or "circus" in any of his advertising or promotional materials or when speaking to the press. The venture was always referred to as Buffalo Bill's Wild West, until 1893 when it was renamed Buffalo Bill's Wild West and Congress of Rough Riders of the World.

Though many of the reenactments were heavily embellished for entertainment purposes, there was a basis of fact involved in much of the spectacle, such as circling the wagons to fend off bandit and Indian attacks, or "cowboy's fun," which demonstrated real techniques used by ranch hands and cowboys when breaking and corralling horses (a section of the exhibition that eventually led to what we know as the modern-day rodeo). Buffalo Bill also drew inspiration from several trick shooters who were making a name for themselves in the late 1870s—most notably A. H. Bogardus, "Texas" Jack Omohundro, and William Frank "Doc" Carver.

These men incorporated multiple types of stunt shooting in their displays of pistol prowess, including shooting glass balls while on horseback and elaborate target shooting competitions against one another. In fact, Buffalo Bill found so much inspiration from these men, he hired all of them for one purpose or another. Texas Jack acted alongside Cody in the first Wild West stage performance titled "Scouts of the Prairie," written by the novelist Ned Buntline. Bogardus and his sons toured with Cody for a year in Buffalo Bill's Wild West. And in the case of Doc Carver, he is credited for helping Cody bring the Wild West out of its infancy and into reality in 1883. Unfortunately for Cody and Carver, the two had a falling out. But Bill never forgot any of these men and implemented the influence each man offered into his historic enterprise.

Another influence on the creation of the Wild West was dime novels. In 1860 publishers Erastus and Irwin Beadle released a new series of cheap paperbacks, Beadle's Dime Novels.[21] These short stories soon became popular and best-selling items. They featured frontiersmen and soldiers riding to the rescue, fighting bandits, and solving crimes, and occasionally had a touch of science fiction in them.

One of the more successful authors of dime novels was Edward Zane Carroll Judson, who is more commonly known by his pseudonym, Ned Buntline. In 1869, while giving lectures on temperance, Buntline rode a train from California to Nebraska and met Buffalo Bill Cody.[22] The two men soon became friends and Buntline decided he would write a novel featuring Cody as the titular character titled *Buffalo Bill, the King of the Border Men*. The success of this novel eventually led to Bill's acting career, and the influence of this storytelling format remained with Bill throughout his time as a showman.

In the pages of these novels, Bill saw himself portrayed as an almost superhuman being who could take on entire bands of marauders and single-handedly save the day. He was all knowing, all powerful, and always just in his causes. Bill would eventually incorporate many of these same characteristics into the character he portrayed in his Wild West.

It is true that Buffalo Bill would often inject himself into his show's "historic reenactments" ("The First Scalp for Custer," etc.). And it is also true he always seemed to be the hero at the outcome of these portrayals. Bill's reputation was built through stories in dime novels, nickel weeklies, and acting in stage performances before he ever created his Wild West show. Bill also had experience as a scout and buffalo hunter, and had fought in numerous conflicts during the Indian Wars.

Unlike many hucksters of the period, Bill never forgot his experiences on the Great Plains. William Cody's influences were wide ranging when it came to inspiration for Buffalo Bill's Wild West. He focused on his own real-life experiences, he borrowed from charlatans like P. T. Barnum, he was open to new ideas and interpretations he gleaned from men like Doc Carver and Texas Jack, and he used his knowledge of the theater and his place as a character in dime novels to build his reputation. This soup of ideas and influences eventually led to one of the greatest entertainment spectacles this country has ever known, Buffalo Bill's Wild West!

CHAPTER 2
Experiences Make the Man

"Among the most noted and daring riders of the Pony Express was Hon. William F. Cody, better known as Buffalo Bill, whose reputation is now established the world over."[1] These words slowly slipped from Alexander Majors's lips and made their way to the ears of biographer and dime novelist Prentiss Ingraham, who scrawled them down for Majors's memoir, *Seventy Years on the Frontier*. Originally published in 1893, Majors and Ingraham worked feverishly to produce a memoir describing Alexander's time as a founding partner of Russell, Majors, and Waddell Freighting and Staging Company, which was the parent company of the historic Pony Express.

Working alongside his partners William Hepburn Russell and William B. Waddell, Alexander Majors formed the Pony Express mail service on April 3, 1860. Not long after its founding, however, the Pony went out of business, in October 1861. Following the failure of the Pony, the demise of its parent company took place only a few months later, in March 1862.[2]

Although the Pony Express was short lived, tales of riders braving arduous journeys through hostile Indian country to heroically deliver the mail on time abounded, allowing it to become one of the most well-remembered, mythologized, and romanticized enterprises in the annals of western history. The reason the Pony is ingrained in the consciousness of so many Americans today, however, is due to the efforts of one man, William Frederick "Buffalo Bill" Cody.

After selling his farming land in 1853 in rural Scott County, Iowa, Isaac Cody, Bill's father, moved his family to Fort Leavenworth, Kansas Territory. Isaac, who was

Buffalo Bill as a young frontiersman, circa 1870

a staunch abolitionist during the lead-up to the Civil War, found himself embroiled in fierce political debates with many of the pro-slavery people living in Kansas Territory. On one occasion, when Isaac was delivering a speech on abolitionism at a trading post, a pro-slavery faction of men drove a bowie knife into his chest several times, severely injuring him.[3]

The Cody patriarch initially survived the wound but later succumbed to the injury after developing a respiratory infection in 1857. Left without a father, Bill, as one of seven siblings, had to help provide for his family.[4] At the tender age of eleven, Bill took a job as a "boy extra" with a freighter company. This job required him to ride on horseback up and down the wagon train of freighters delivering messages between the drivers and workmen. It was not long before Cody joined Colonel Albert Sidney Johnston's army. Albert Sidney led a combined US force to put down a rumored rebellion by the Mormon population of Salt Lake City. Cody worked as an unofficial member of the scouts assigned to guide the army to Utah.[5]

To bring in more money for his destitute family, Cody claimed, as a thirteen-year-old boy, to have gone prospecting for gold near Pikes Peak in Colorado Territory. With his knees deep in water and muck, Cody found Colorado's streams and rivers dry of gold. Drenched and discouraged, young Cody cleaned the filth from his trousers and wandered into a Pony Express station in the nearby frontier town of Julesburg.[6] It was there that a boyish fourteen-year-old Bill supposedly answered an advertisement for the mail carrier.

Once joining the Pony, Bill rode a route spanning 116 miles between Red Buttes and Three Crossings in Wyoming Territory.[7] Legend has it that during one of his rides, Buffalo Bill experienced a situation that would help build his reputation and remain part of his legend throughout his lifetime. Riding his steed hard over rough and dangerous terrain, Cody and his horse worked up a good lather following the lonely trail leading to a perilous crossing point on the North Platte River. He crossed the raging river, which in places was nearly twelve feet deep, and continued toward his appointed stop. Hustling at a clip of fifteen miles per hour, Cody reached Three Crossings on time, only to find that the carrier who was to take the mail from him had been killed on the road the previous night. Cody's ready and willing spirit compelled him to act, and he accepted the challenge of carrying the mail another seventy-six miles.[8]

After gulping down a meal, Bill hopped back on his horse and hit the dusty trail. He reached the station at Rocky Ridge, Wyoming Territory, on time with the mail

Pony Express Rider *by William Henry Jackson*

intact. All told, he covered 322 miles with his only stops being for food and a fresh horse.[9] This was one of the greatest feats of endurance ever performed by a Pony rider and is widely considered to be the third-longest Express journey made by any mail carrier.[10]

These descriptions of Bill's time with the Pony Express are drawn directly from Alexander Majors's memoir. However, it has been noted by Cody's detractors that Majors's reminiscences were ghostwritten by Prentiss Ingraham, who was the author of many dime novels starring Buffalo Bill. It is also true that Cody sought out Majors in his old age to put pen to paper and recount his experiences. But Bill's accounts of his time with the Pony have a ring of truth to them, unlike many of the often over-exaggerated tales told by men who claimed to have ridden for the mail service.[11]

Along with that, one of the main points providing credence to Cody's claims as a Pony rider is the fact that a reenactment of the Pony Express was an absolute hallmark of Buffalo Bill's Wild West for decades. Until the consistent portrayal of the Pony in Cody's show, the mail service was thought of as little more than a historical footnote. It was the continued presence of the Pony Express in Buffalo Bill's Wild West that has ingrained the enterprise in the hearts and minds of so many people.

When the Pony Express gave up the ghost in 1861, Bill eventually found work six years later with the Kansas Pacific Railroad providing buffalo meat for the workmen laying the rails. During his time as a hunter, Cody supposedly killed 4,280 bison. Although this is a staggering number of kills to be sure, there were literally millions of the woolly animals still roaming the plains when Bill hung up his holster as the West's premier buffalo slayer. In fact, it would not be until several years after Cody's retirement when the majestic beasts were virtually hunted to extinction by profiteers selling buffalo pelts and tongues for profit across the country.[12]

Cody's prowess with a pistol and rifle, however, helped him cut down many of these majestic creatures and earned him his "Buffalo Bill" nickname. But more importantly, it was his experience riding the range and tracking and hunting bison that eventually led him to incorporate the buffalo hunt in his Wild West performances, employing live bison.

Before Bill was a buffalo hunter, however, he was no stranger to military service. In 1863, at the age of seventeen, he enlisted as a teamster with the rank of private in Company H of the Seventh Kansas Cavalry, serving until honorably discharged in 1865.[13] After the Kansas Pacific Railroad closed up shop with completion of the railroad,

William F. Cody reenacting the buffalo hunt, circa 1900

Bill's time as a buffalo hunter ended. Fortunately for Cody he was not unemployed for long, finding his way back into military service in 1868, this time as a dispatch courier. Because of his superb performance in this position, young Cody became the chief of scouts for the US Fifth Cavalry, where he served during the already raging Indian Wars.

In May 1869 Buffalo Bill would act as scout for a battalion of the Fifth Cavalry marching from Fort Lyon, Colorado Territory, to their new headquarters at Fort McPherson, Nebraska. Commanded by Colonel Eugene Carr, the battalion set out to retaliate against the Cheyenne Dog Soldiers and their leader, Tall Bull. The Fifth Cavalry sought to confront these warriors because they were massacring settlers and freighters across the plains of northern Kansas Territory.[14]

The Dog Soldiers were one of six Cheyenne warrior societies whose members often opposed policies of many of the Cheyenne peace chiefs. During their height, they were both feared and revered for their fighting abilities and their brutal aggression in combat. They often proved their mettle by dismounting during combat, refusing to retreat, and staking themselves to the ground, typically using an arrow by burying the head in the earth, then tying a buffalo-hide sash or "dog rope" to their leg and the other end to the arrow.[15]

Tall Bull, who was one of the chiefs of the Southern Cheyenne, had assumed control of the Dog Soldiers and commanded nearly 450 warriors. During one of their raids, the Dog Soldiers kidnapped three German immigrants: Maria Weichell, Susanna Alderdice, and Susanna's baby. The Dog Soldiers murdered the baby by strangling the infant, then they dragged the women to their encampment.[16]

After learning of this heinous affair, Carr mobilized his troops, which included brothers Luther North and Major Frank North (a translator), several Pawnee Indian scouts, and Buffalo Bill. A day before they departed to engage the Dog Soldiers, the cavalry troops paraded at the fort, performing mock charges with sabers drawn. The Pawnee scouts matched the display by making mock charges of their own. After these festivities, the Pawnee departed to spend the night performing their war dances and recitation of personal battle histories.[17] Seeing this spectacular sight, it is easy to imagine Buffalo Bill being influenced by the traditions of those native warriors, whom he eventually incorporated into the performances of his Wild West.

The following day the Fifth Cavalry skirmished with the Dog Soldiers along with some Sioux warriors who had joined forces with the Cheyenne militants.[18] After several minor engagements many of the soldiers' mounts were exhausted. So Colonel Carr selected 244 soldiers, 50 Pawnee scouts, the North brothers, and Buffalo Bill to track and attack the Dog Soldiers.[19]

Following the lead of the Pawnee scouts, Cody and the rest of Carr's column were able to track Tall Bull and his soldiers to an encampment known as Summit Springs, just south of present-day Sterling, Colorado. Riding in three columns the cavalry charged with guns blazing, and pandemonium ensued. The soldiers and Pawnee scouts fell upon the Cheyenne hostiles with speed, precision, and ferocity.[20]

The Pawnee warriors, noted for the quickness at which they arrived in the Cheyenne village, were particularly bloody in their aggression during the battle. They claimed several Dog Soldier lives but also fell upon numerous unarmed combatants, killing and wounding several Cheyenne women and children. Buffalo Bill, for his part in the fracas, perched himself on a ridge with his Winchester rifle and fired at any number of Dog Soldiers attempting to escape the fight. In doing so, Cody killed an Indian who was apparently riding Tall Bull's prized painted pony. After the battle Cody was attributed with killing the Dog Soldier chief Tall Bull.[21]

All in all, the battle ended as quickly as it began. The Fifth Cavalry recorded deaths of fifty-two Dog Soldiers, including their leader Tall Bull, and the capture of seventeen Cheyenne hostages. Some other sources recorded thirty-five Dog Soldiers killed. The Fifth Cavalry escaped with only one man wounded. As for the captives, Maria Weichell received a life-threatening injury but survived, while Susanna Alderdice was murdered by a Dog Soldier the moment the battle began.[22]

This rout by the Fifth Cavalry became known as the Battle of Summit Springs and would mark the end of hostilities on the plains of Colorado Territory. After this fight the Dog Soldiers fragmented into two groups, one drifting north to join the Northern Cheyenne and the other joining the Southern Cheyenne. Neither would be a threat again.[23]

In the years following the battle, Buffalo Bill would claim he killed Chief Tall Bull, but most historians speculate the man Cody shot from his horse was a brave who had taken Tall Bull's horse in an attempt to flee the fight.[24] Either way, Bill received military honors for his service during the engagement and, more importantly, he would reenact the battle as part of his Wild West show.

Three Sioux men pose on horseback in a camp for Buffalo Bill's Wild West Show, 1901.

Another influential experience during Buffalo Bill's time on the frontier came in 1876, the year of America's Centennial. While continuing to scout for the Fifth Cavalry, Cody engaged in perhaps his most famous fight during the Indian Wars. Following the destruction of General George Armstrong Custer's Seventh Cavalry troops at the Battle of the Little Bighorn in Montana Territory, reports of their demise eventually reached Buffalo Bill and the Fifth Cavalry on July 7.[25]

Initially the Fifth Cavalry received word that eight hundred Cheyenne Indians had deserted the Red Cloud and Spotted Tail Agencies in Nebraska. They were supposedly led by Chief Little Wolf, and apparently these Cheyenne had every intention of joining Sitting Bull, Crazy Horse, and the rest of the Sioux nation on the warpath. Shortly after receiving word of Custer's defeat, the Fifth Cavalry became determined to not allow any of these Cheyenne to join the rampaging Sioux.[26]

Again acting as a scout, Buffalo Bill was able to guide Colonel Wesley Merritt's 350 Fifth Cavalry troops to a position where they could intercept the Cheyenne. Merritt planned an ambush by camouflaging most of his troopers inside covered wagons and posting sharpshooters nearby. Spotting Merritt's seemingly unescorted wagon train along Warbonnet Creek, a small war party of six Cheyenne warriors charged directly into the trap to divert attention from the main body of Cheyenne. Most of those Indians, seeing the strength and size of the Fifth Cavalry, retreated to their agencies as a small skirmish took place between the troops and the backpedaling Indians.[27] It is here that Buffalo Bill solidified his status as a formidable frontiersman.

According to legend, Bill, dressed in a stage costume of black velvet trimmed with silver buttons, challenged a young Cheyenne sub-chief named Yellow Hair (often mistranslated as Yellow Hand).[28] The account, according to Cody, had Yellow Hair riding to the front of his braves, rising up on his steed and calling out to Cody, saying, "I know you, Pa-he-haska, if you want to fight, come ahead and fight me."[29] Pa-he-haska or Pahaska is translated from the Sioux language as meaning Long Hair, which is the name the Sioux gave to Buffalo Bill for his flowing locks.

Bill, in turn, accepted the challenge and barreled toward the charging Cheyenne warrior. Driving their horseflesh hard, the two men fired simultaneously. Cody's bullet traveled true, finding purchase and burying itself in Yellow Hair's horse. The Cheyenne's bullet went astray, but Bill fell to the earth anyway as his horse stepped into a gopher hole. Both combatants scrambled to their feet, and again both men fired at

"The first scalp for Custer"; Cody's battle with Yellow Hair

each other. Cody again would come out on top, with his bullet hitting Yellow Hair squarely while the Indians again went wild.[30]

Falling to the earth as life left his body, Yellow Hair lay motionless on the battlefield. Cody then walked up to the fallen warrior and claimed his scalp, peeling it from the Indian's head with his hunting knife. Raising the bloody trophy in triumph, Cody shouted, "The first scalp for Custer!"[31]

This, however, is a heavily fictionalized version of events. Buffalo Bill, at the time, was already crafting a stage persona, having acted in multiple plays. It is true that he scouted with the Fifth Infantry then and did help them ambush the Cheyenne fleeing the agencies in Nebraska. However, he most likely encountered the Cheyenne brave Yellow Hair by accident when he was racing to warn two couriers about a potential counter-ambush by the Cheyenne. It is here that Bill did in fact best the brave in hand-to-hand combat, just not as dramatically as it was retold.[32]

After the death of Yellow Hair, the main body of warriors eventually attempted to rescue the small war party but fled quickly after seeing the true strength of the US forces. A few warriors were wounded by the troopers, but the main engagement of the battle was the duel between Buffalo Bill and Yellow Hair.[33]

With Yellow Hair's scalp in hand, Cody later mailed the gory trophy home to his wife, Louisa. Attached to the three-inch-square scrap of decayed flesh was a swath of straight black hair reportedly two feet long. Bill also kept Yellow Hair's headdress made from buffalo skin and adorned in eagle feathers. He also claimed Yellow Hair's shield that was itself adorned in human scalps.[34]

All these items, combined with Bill's embellished tale of his duel with Yellow Hair, served as great publicity material for his burgeoning stage career. And ever the showman, Buffalo Bill never missed the opportunity to capitalize on his grizzly war trophy, wrapping it around tales of the western frontier.[35]

When Bill returned to the stage, his show was highlighted by a melodramatic reenactment of his duel with Yellow Hair. He displayed the fallen warrior's scalp, feather warbonnet, knife, saddle, and other personal effects. He later celebrated the killing during his Wild West shows in a reenactment he titled "The Red Right Hand, or, Buffalo Bill's First Scalp for Custer."[36]

Cody had been appearing on stage since 1872. And while Bill was creating his stage persona, he also continued his scouting for the military. The duel with Yellow

Hair was a singularly important event for him and helped influence many of his future proceedings. The duel lent credence to Bill's role as the heroic plainsman on the playhouse stage as well as on history's stage.

CHAPTER 3

From Prairie to Playhouse

In 1872, at the same time Cody was riding the range, fighting Indians, and hunting buffalo, he made his acting debut. Four years before Bill's foray on the theater stage however, Cody, by chance, met an author who went by the pen name Ned Buntline. It was a fortuitous encounter that would propel Bill toward superstardom.

Ned Buntline, whose real name was Edward Zane Carroll Judsen, was born in Harpersfield, New York, in 1821. Earlier in his career, Buntline served as a US Navy midshipman during the Seminole Wars, seeing little to no action. During the Civil War, Buntline enlisted in the First New York Mounted Rifles, where he acquired the rank of sergeant before being discharged for drunkenness.[1] Finding his military career aspirations dashed, Ned decided to try his hand in the publishing business.

After failing as a publisher, Buntline began writing sensationalistic fiction stories for multiple newspapers. As a supplement to his writing income, and in a rather humorous turn for a man expelled from the military for overimbibing, the portly writer began giving lectures on temperance and the evils of alcohol to sobriety leagues around the country.[2] His talks would eventually bring Buntline and Cody into the same sphere.

There are many conflicting accounts as to how exactly Buntline and Cody first met. But one of the most interesting versions begins with Buntline boarding a train heading to his home in New York after having given a temperance lecture in California. While riding the train, he supposedly made one of the greatest discoveries in the history of the entertainment industry.

Buntline originally was looking to write a story on the noted gunfighter Wild Bill Hickok after reading about him in a greatly embellished article in *Harper's New Monthly Magazine*. The article covered Hickok's supposed gunfight with David McCanles at Rock Creek Station in Nebraska. Buntline envisioned himself stopping in Nebraska on his way back to New York and scooping a story with the heralded gunfighter. Unfortunately for Ned, Hickok put an end to this notion in short order. Legend has it that when Buntline stopped in Fort McPherson, Nebraska, he found the steely-eyed gunfighter in a saloon. Apparently, Buntline burst into the bar and, seeing Wild Bill, shouted, "There's my man! I want you!" In response the lawman drew down on the novelist with a loaded six-shooter and ordered him to get his keister out of town by the end of the day.[3]

After being rebuffed by Hickok, Buntline dejectedly climbed back onto the train with his head hung low. But no sooner had he found his seat when he came upon Buffalo Bill Cody, who was riding the train with a group of men returning from a skirmish with Cheyenne Indians.[4] Greeting the pathfinder with a hearty shake of the hand, the rotund Buntline became enamored with Cody. Buntline's adoration of Bill is perhaps due to Bill being everything he was not. Cody's flowing locks, good looks, confident demeanor, and all-around charisma set him apart from most men. Whatever the case, the moment he met Cody, Buntline knew he had found the next subject for his sensational stories.

Cody, who became instant friends with Buntline, would be the centerpiece of Ned's new serialized novel *Buffalo Bill, King of the Bordermen*, first published on December 23, 1869, in the *New York Weekly*.[5] With the success of this fictional tale, playhouse producers were soon contacting Buntline to adapt the story for the stage. When the play initially debuted, an actor named J. B. Studley portrayed Buffalo Bill.[6]

During one of the performances, however, Cody decided to attend and see how well his life story was being received. When the audience realized they had a living legend sitting among them, they implored Cody to take the stage and speak. After Cody stepped into the spotlight, he stumbled over his words and stammered out a mostly inaudible response to the adoring onlookers.[7]

Even though Bill mumbled his way through his first appearance on center stage, Buntline became convinced Cody had star power potential. In 1872 Ned persuaded Bill to take up acting. Adding to the hype surrounding the freshly minted actor, in January of the same year Cody received a large amount of national renown when he

Ned Buntline, Buffalo Bill, and Texas Jack Omohundro

led Russia's Grand Duke Alexis and General George Armstrong Custer on a hunting expedition. During the hunt, Cody demonstrated how Indians tracked buffalo and gave the Grand Duke a personal shooting lesson. Word of the incredible event soon reached the press and made Cody a recognizable figure on the national stage.[8]

The much-publicized hunt and his decision to become an actor was a piece of for-tuitous timing on Cody's part. In what became a hastily cobbled together production written by Buntline a week before its opening, *Scouts of the Prairie, and Red Deviltry as It Is* debuted in Chicago. Buffalo Bill appeared in his first role alongside fellow fron-tiersman Texas Jack Omohundro and numerous American Indians.[9]

Cody and Texas Jack bumbled their way through every scene, forgetting their lines, fidgeting with their hands, and not remembering their stage directions. In fact, Bill became so confused at one point that he stopped trying to say his lines and began recounting a well-publicized hunting trip he had guided with a well-known Chicago resident named Milligan whom he saw sitting in the audience. The spectators cheered the moment in hopes Cody would share new tidbits about the expedition.[10]

Capitalizing on his popularity among the public, Cody soon formed what he referred to as "Buffalo Bill's Combination." This "combination" was a troupe of actors who toured all over the country, going from theater to theater putting on stage perfor-mances, very much in the same vein as a circus.[11]

Traditionally the theater was maintained by permanent companies supplying reliable, classically trained actors. These men and women had the skills to perform in many roles, whether comedy, drama, or action adventure. These productions also included numerous stage stars who brought clout to the performances.

When it came to Buffalo Bill's troupe, however, Cody carried most of the shows by himself, usually emphasizing his dual careers as a scout and showman. These plays were normally accompanied by few other professional actors. Though the shows were almost universally panned by reviewers and newspaper critics, audiences arrived in droves to see them and became enamored by Cody's presence on stage. Performing to packed playhouses, it was almost as if the people in attendance were aware that they were witnessing the birth of a legend.[12]

In 1873, economic depression spread throughout most of Europe and the United States from multiple circumstances including the collapse of the American railroad industry and the German Empire's discontinuation of mining silver, which depressed silver prices around the world. This financial hardship affected many Americans, and as a result numerous traveling show combinations closed their doors. Buffalo Bill's Combination, however, survived. This is truly a testament to Cody's staying power and his popularity, and an example of how he would eventually reach international fame.

Amazingly, during that same year, the man whom Ned Buntline originally sought to write about in 1869, Wild Bill Hickok, joined Buffalo Bill's Combination as a star attraction. Cody and Hickok were already acquainted, having worked together as freighters on the Great Plains. During that time Bill saw Hickok as a mentor and eventually credited Wild Bill with helping him develop his frontiersman skills. Already a recognized and much written about figure because of his exploits as a lawman and gunfighter, Hickok made a great addition to Buffalo Bill's popular show. Unfortunately, Wild Bill did not last long with the production.[13]

Apparently, Hickok did not relish his stage experiences. He was gruff in many of his interactions with the other performers. He supposedly shot too near some of the actors' legs during one of the productions. And it is also reported he shot out the house lights when he did not get enough of the spotlight.[14]

According to all involved, if Cody's acting left something to be desired, Hickok's was beyond atrocious. He did not recite lines coherently and could not remember stage directions, and his eyesight had begun to fail, so he constantly incurred problems with the house lights. Hickok also had never aspired to be a solid showman like his companion Cody and eventually left the company in March 1874. After his departure, Hickok's role in the show was filled by a professional actor. Hickok returned to the Great Plains, but a little more than two years later, in 1876, he was shot and killed by Jack McCall during a poker game in Deadwood, Dakota Territory.[15]

In the same year as Wild Bill's death, Cody's other counterpart, Texas Jack Omohundro, left Buffalo Bill's traveling troupe after just three seasons.[16] Omohundro would go on to act in several more shows and achieve a moderate level of success. In Bill's Combination, he was soon replaced by actor Jack Crawford. Omohundro married one of the actresses from the Bill's Combination, Giuseppina Morrlacchi, and the two eventually settled in Massachusetts. Sadly, for Texas Jack, he would die from pneumonia in 1880, four years after leaving Bill's Combination.[17]

Interestingly, several individuals who became major players in Buffalo Bill's Wild West had also served in some capacity in his Combination. One of these individuals was "Arizona" John Burke, who was also known as Major John Burke. Born in 1842 in

New York City, Burke made a trek out West to Montana Territory, where he became acquainted with Buffalo Bill Cody. He was soon hired as Cody's assistant when Bill was the chief of scouts for the US Fifth Cavalry.[18]

Although he used the military rank of "Major" and the nickname "Arizona" as interchangeable titles, Burke never had any association with either. He was never in the military and he never had any connection with the state or territory of Arizona. Though Burke embellished his heading, he was an innovator in the art of promotion and an important piece in helping build the legacy of the Wild West show.

Burke followed Bill from the prairie to the playhouse, handling most of the publicity for the play *The Scouts of the Prairie*. After Texas Jack Omohundro and Buffalo Bill amicably parted ways, Burke took over as Texas Jack's manager, working in concert with Ned Buntline, who wrote a serial feature for Omohundro and his wife as well as multiple stage productions for the duo.[19] It is interesting to note that if Omohundro had not succumbed to pneumonia in 1880 he very well might have become as famous as Buffalo Bill. He had the charisma and style that drew audiences to his performances, but unfortunately for Texas Jack it was not meant to be.

Texas Jack certainly had excellent management in Arizona John, an experienced author producing his plays in Buntline, and a great acting counterpart in Giuseppina. Their real-life marriage helped add believability to their stage performances. Burke, after the death of Omohundro, eventually returned to the frontier fold, teaming up with Cody and becoming his publicity manager. Burke's innovation in promotion and advertising was instrumental in helping Buffalo Bill become a household name.

Another relationship that helped Buffalo Bill reach national fame was that of Captain Jack Crawford. Cody and Crawford originally met during the Great Sioux War. In September 1876, Crawford gained national recognition for his role in the Battle of Slim Buttes in Dakota Territory. After the battle ended, Crawford rode 350 miles to Fort Laramie in six days carrying news of General George Crook's victory against the Sioux Indians. During his time in Dakota Territory, Crawford supposedly delivered a bottle of whisky to Buffalo Bill, who was scouting in the area.[20]

After gaining some national acclaim for his ride, Crawford decided to try his hand at acting and found work with Buffalo Bill and his Combination later in 1876. It is well documented that the men were originally friends, and Cody even mentioned Crawford's famous ride in his autobiography. Unfortunately for the two men, their friendship soured in the summer of 1877 in Virginia City, Nevada.[21]

Major "Arizona" John Burke, 1890

During a stage performance in which there was a horseback combat scene staged with Buffalo Bill, Jack received an injury after accidentally being shot in the groin. Captain Jack initially said he accidentally shot himself during the performance, but later he focused the blame for the wound on Cody. Jack accused Bill of being in a drunken stupor when he flippantly fired a round into Crawford's crotch. Jack was confined to bed for more than two weeks.[22] This incident would signal the end of the friendship between the two men, and Jack would not forgive Cody for supposedly shooting him in the nether regions. The loss of this friendship would later have an impact on Cody's career.

One of the other key factors assisting Bill's rise in public recognition was the changing functions of mass media. Many of the national newspapers with the highest circulations began manufacturing stories to fill their newspaper pages. Instead of just reporting the news, these companies began sending their reporters to root out celebrity gossip. Some of the more adventurous journalists even injected themselves into the stories they were covering.[23] Buffalo Bill and Major Burke took full advantage of this new type of celebrity journalism.

It is perhaps difficult for modern audiences to truly grasp the uniqueness of Cody's career as a showman. In today's entertainment landscape, many of the actors and actresses seen on the big screen or on television have had no other career than that of a thespian. Many of these individuals began acting as children, pushed into the pursuit by overzealous parents. Or in many instances they were by-products of an industry rife with nepotism—the children and grandchildren of people who have worked in the show business industry for generations.

In the case of Buffalo Bill, however, here was a man participating in military missions against hostile Indians on the Great Plains or leading hunting expeditions with General George Custer and then in the same month treading on the boards of a stage, wowing audiences across the nation with his "blood and thunder" Western melodramas. Cody truly was the closest thing to a living legend the entertainment industry will ever know.

Perhaps one of the only modern equivalents to Buffalo Bill that comes to mind is the decorated war-hero-turned-actor Audie Murphy. Murphy, like Cody, received a Medal of Honor for service to his country. Unlike Cody, however, Murphy ended his military career and narrowed his focus on his acting ambitions. Cody, meanwhile, continued to serve as a civilian scout for the military while establishing himself as a star on the stage.

One of the people who would usher in Cody's meteoric rise was an author named Prentiss Ingraham. Prentiss was an interesting individual in his own right. At the time he became acquainted with Buffalo Bill, Ingraham had already served in the Confederate Army and achieved the rank of colonel. He also had a brief career as a mercenary traveling to Mexico, where he fought with Benito Juárez against the French.[24]

Ingraham had also seen action across the globe during the Battle of Sadowa, Austria, in 1866, and had been in Crete fighting the Turks and in Khedive's army in Egypt. In 1869 he fought alongside the Cuban rebels against Spain. This last venture, however, saw him captured by the Spanish and condemned to death, but he eventually escaped.[25]

In the same year Ingraham escaped the Spanish noose, his literary career blossomed in London. Prentiss wrote his first story, *The Masked Spy*, in 1872, and by the end of his career he claimed to have authored more than six hundred novels.[26] However, Prentiss would become most well-known for his series of dime novels featuring Buffalo Bill Cody. Ingraham and Cody first became acquainted in the 1870s when Ingraham wrote the play *The Red Right Hand; or, Buffalo Bill's First Scalp for Custer*, which was a loose retelling of Cody's killing of Yellow Hair. Most historians credit Ingraham for reimagining the Yellow Hair fight as a duel of honor between the Indian warrior and Cody.[27] Ingraham is also credited with ghostwriting many of the thirteen novels that Buffalo Bill took credit for, which helped further fuel Cody's reputation.[28]

During his time on stage, however, Cody's brain began bubbling with greater ambition. It is reported Cody first conceived of Buffalo Bill's Wild West in 1882 and wanted to enter a partnership with well-known actor and entertainment manager Nate Salsbury. Salsbury was born in 1846 in Rockport, Illinois. He served in the Union Army during the Civil War with the 15th Illinois Volunteer Infantry Regiment. After being injured in battle and subsequently discharged, Salsbury re-upped for military service, joining the 89th Illinois Regiment, and saw fierce combat at the Battles of Chickamauga and Chattanooga.[29]

After the end of the Civil War, Salsbury studied banking and finance at Illinois Business College. Short on cash, he tried out for a spot in a play titled *Pocahontas*. He won the role, but the play shuttered its doors after the first evening's performance. Although his first acting experience was short lived, Salsbury continued to pursue show business. He spent four years performing in comedies on the stage of the Boston Museum in the early 1870s. He formed Nate Salsbury's Troubadours (a stock

Nate Salsbury in England, 1887

company) and in 1879 wrote and performed in *The Brook; or, A Jolly Day at the Picnic*, which is considered by many to be the first musical comedy.[30]

Throughout the 1870s, Salsbury worked hard to hone his craft as an actor and achieved a good deal of success with his Troubadours. Although Bill and Salsbury's partnership did not come to fruition in the fledgling year of Buffalo Bill's Wild West, the two would eventually make a connection two years later, forming an alliance that became a smashing success.

In the meantime Bill found a business counterpart in the form of a man named William Frank "Doc" Carver. Doc was an acquaintance of Bill's from his time in Fort McPherson, Nebraska. Carver had met both Cody and Texas Jack Omohundro while Bill was working for the Kansas Pacific Railroad and guiding bison hunts. "Doc" was a nickname Carver invented for himself, claiming he acquired it from Indians who called him "The Great Bad Medicine" because of his deadly accuracy with a rifle.[31]

Like Salsbury, Carver was born in Illinois sometime in the 1840s. Little is known about his early life, but it is known that he moved to the western frontier in 1872. While working as a dentist in Nebraska, Doc learned to hunt, ride horseback, and, most importantly, target shoot. Carver worked feverishly on his marksmanship, improving his prowess with a pistol and rifle until he could hit the bullseye of any target. Because his abilities as a sharpshooter were far better than his skills with the drill and hook as a dentist, Carver took up target shooting as a full-time occupation. His considerable talents with a gun afforded him audiences with several entertainment enterprises, and it was not long before he was making a living with his shooting skills.[32]

Much like Buffalo Bill, Carver embellished parts of his early life and encounters on the frontier. Unlike Buffalo Bill, however, there was no amount of truth in his tales and most of his stories were total fabrication, including his tales about being captured by Sioux Indians. Carver claimed he was kidnapped by the Sioux as a young boy, but they became so impressed with his shooting skill and his lust for revenge that they dubbed him "Evil Spirit of the Plains" upon releasing him. Though he was a big blowhard, Carver would soon become an integral piece of Buffalo Bill's Wild West.[33]

Through the cultivation of these numerous friendships, it was as though Cody could sense the brewing storm. Events, relationships, and opportunities were all aligning themselves to allow Bill to capitalize on an idea that would send his fame into the stratosphere. His experiences on the stage and in front of adoring crowds, along with the men who influenced him, all helped Buffalo Bill prepare for the second half of his career.

CHAPTER 4

The Launch of a Legend and the Loss of a Friend

When historians write about the beginning of Buffalo Bill's Wild West, there is always one name that repeatedly crops up, William Frank "Doc" Carver. Doc met Buffalo Bill in 1874 when Cody was hired to guide English gent Thomas Medley on a hunting expedition in Nebraska. Carver, who was living in the area, accompanied the group.[1]

After the hunt, Cody returned to his career in the theater and Carver began to hone his sharpshooting skills. Doc soon set several sharpshooting records in Europe and the United States. Word of his reputation with a rifle began to spread, eventually reaching the ear of Buffalo Bill. Meanwhile, as Bill's stage career began to flourish, Cody found he wanted to expand his sights beyond the stage by creating an outdoor extravaganza celebrating the history of the Old West.[2]

P. T. Barnum's circus attractions had already proven American audiences had a taste for outdoor acts incorporating livestock and actors with exciting high-flying events. So, on July 4, 1882, Buffalo Bill produced what at the time was titled the "Old Glory Blowout." This undertaking was an extremely successful event featuring examples of exhibitions that would come to populate Buffalo Bill's Wild West.[3] The event received glowing reviews with the *Omaha Bee* noting, "Buffalo Bill has certainly out-Barnumed Barnum in his novel show."[4]

In January 1883, while in New Haven, Connecticut, where Carver was living at the time, Buffalo Bill paid his old acquaintance a visit and asked Doc if he wanted to partner in an enterprise that would eventually become Buffalo Bill's Wild West. Even though the well-known actor Nate Salsbury first brought the idea to Cody's attention

Full-length portrait of Doc William F. Carver standing with rifle across his shoulders. Photographer A. H. Arnold, circa 1880.

Photo courtesy of the Buffalo Bill Center of the West

in 1882, it was Carver who received the chance to partner with Cody. This initial rejection by Buffalo Bill left a sour taste in Nate Salsbury's mouth for quite some time. However, he eventually got over it.[5]

When Carver and Cody first began to share their ideas of what the spectacle would entail, they came up with several different names for the show. Both men liked the title "Wild West," but Carver was also fond of the name "Golden West," which his brother-in-law Hugh Dailey originally suggested. In fact, several newspapers initially reported Cody and Carver were going to name their enterprise "The Golden West."[6]

After sketching out the initial details of the business venture, Cody traveled to North Platte, Nebraska, and began using his own cash to build up a stable of actors and livestock. He also purchased the Deadwood Stagecoach, which, interestingly, would eventually become as synonymous with the Wild West as Buffalo Bill or Annie Oakley. During the time Cody was compiling the Wild West troupe, Carver remained on the East Coast participating in shooting competitions against his nemesis Captain Adam Henry Bogardus. Bogardus was a world-champion trap shooter as well as the inventor of the first practical glass ball trap. Bogardus would join Cody and Carver's Wild West in 1883, becoming the main sharpshooter for the enterprise.[7]

When Carver arrived in Nebraska later in 1883 to help Cody with the show, he found the name had changed from "Carver and Cody's Golden West" to "Cody and Carver's Wild West." There is no indication Carver protested the name change. This was most likely due to the fact Cody was already well-known throughout the country and Carver had little if any name recognition among the public.[8]

The first official show in Cody and Carver's Wild West launched on May 19, 1883, at the Omaha fairgrounds. The show received excellent reviews, with Cody garnering most of the accolades. This praise, however, angered an already jealous Doc Carver, who began sniping at Buffalo Bill as the 1883 season wore on. Carver initially complained that Cody was drunk much of the summer and unable to deal with the business's requirements.[9]

This accusation proved to be quite hypocritical, as Carver was known to over-indulge in alcoholic beverages quite frequently and was often unable to handle his own affairs let alone the affairs of the Wild West. Other extenuating circumstances also added to the feuding between the two men. During the 1883 season, Buffalo Bill found it increasingly difficult to manage the Wild West finances and scheduling of shows while trying to keep his actors and livestock prepped for the performances.

Captain Adam Henry Bogardus (center left) and "Doc" William Frank Carver (center right) standing among a crowd of people at a shooting match, circa 1890.
Photo courtesy of the Buffalo Bill Center of the West

Because most of the day-to-day operations were thrust upon Cody's back, it became quite difficult for him to balance everything while Carver showed little interest in the day-to-day operations.[10]

This stress coupled with the constant griping of the egotistical Carver brought the entire situation to a boil for Buffalo Bill in October 1883. Cody and Carver decided to mutually dissolve the enterprise after the two had a disagreement when Carver demanded to take the show on a winter tour. At the end of the partnership, each man walked away with an equal share of the assets.[11] Doc took his half of the show and partnered with an old nemesis of Bill's, the actor Jack Crawford, who still harbored hard feelings toward Cody after claiming he had been injured by the scout. Doc and Jack titled their show, "Carver and Crawford's Wild West," and both did their damnedest to sandbag Cody at every turn.[12]

Buffalo Bill, following the dissolution of Cody and Carver's Wild West, took his half of the show and approached Nate Salsbury to start a partnership. Though he was none too happy with having been rebuffed by Bill a year earlier, Salsbury did not pass up the lucrative opportunity. In December 1883, Bill and Nate applied to copyright the "Wild West" narrative, which they eventually completely acquired in 1885.[13] When Salsbury and Cody entered this legal process, it would mark an important moment in the history of the entertainment industry. It allowed Cody to separate his business from the horde of circuses, traveling Indian shows, and other imposter acts popping up at the time.[14]

The following season, in 1884, Cody and Carver unleashed their reorganized shows on the public, setting up performances and traveling across the country putting on competing events. The men would eventually show up in St. Louis a week apart from each other. Prentiss Ingraham, who was acting as Buffalo Bill's press agent, informed the local St. Louis newspapers that Carver was in violation of copyright law as Cody and Salsbury had already copywritten the title "Wild West." Carver disputed the accusation and quickly retitled his enterprise "The Original Wild West." Both shows performed in St. Louis, and after a great deal of legal finagling, both played to crowds numbering in the thousands.[15]

Carver normally tried to undercut Bill at the box office, offering admission fees of twenty-five cents for adults and ten cents for children, while Buffalo Bill set his prices at fifty cents for adults and twenty-five cents for children. Doc also attempted to beat Bill to the punch by arriving in the same town a week, or sometimes just days, before

Buffalo Bill's Wild West was to put on a performance. Cody and Carver continued to throw verbal jabs at each other in the press until Bill eventually brought an injunction against Carver in 1884 over the use of the Wild West name. As the court battle began, both shows continued to put on performances.[16]

In 1885, however, events came to an impasse at the most unlikely of battle-grounds, Connecticut. In July of that year, Cody attached a libel suit to Carver's show for $16,000 and included a writ of attachment on all property relating to Carver's Wild West show. This meant that any of the performance equipment could not travel to the next city and had to stay with Carver until the matter was resolved. The suit was brought against Doc and his outfit when it was discovered his backers had distributed handbills denouncing Cody as a fraud. Cody's people in turn circulated playbills pointing to Carver as the true fraudster.[17]

Doc was eventually arrested and held in Willimantic, Connecticut. This legal action kept Carver from leaving at his scheduled time and forced him to miss several performance engagements. The injunction also kept Carver from rebilling the towns and parks he had previously scheduled, which caused him to lose out on a large portion of income.[18]

Doc's time spent in Willimantic also forced him to spend an extra $2,000 in wages to the men in his employ, who were waiting to receive word as to where Carver's Wild West would head next. After Cody scored this legal victory, each man lawyered up, collecting a council of attorneys. Cody and Salsbury filed another injunction against Carver after the authorities released him on bond. This prevented Doc from trying to show up at prescheduled performing grounds that Cody and Salsbury had already reserved for Buffalo Bill's Wild West. The injunction also prevented Carver from trying to stop Cody's Wild West from proceeding as scheduled for even an hour.[19]

Carver retaliated against the injunction by filing a lawsuit for $25,000 charging Bill with libel, false imprisonment, illegal detention, and malicious prosecution. After some more legal fighting, Buffalo Bill was taken into custody and spent the night in New Haven while his Wild West troupe proceeded to Bridgeport without him. While in a New Haven court for the legal proceedings, Cody offered to pay $16,000 to settle the suit, which was accepted by the presiding judge.[20]

After the amount was paid, Cody headed for Bridgeport. But Carver's lawyers continued to legally wrangle over who rightfully owned the rights to the name "Wild West." After hearing both sides, it was determined by a judge that Cody had to give a deposition about the ownership of the Wild West moniker but that it would not interfere with his current duties performing with his show. It was also decided that an arrest warrant would be issued if Cody did not appear for his deposition.[21]

Cody did show for his deposition, however, and began giving his testimony in the office of a judge named Whedon on the morning of July 16, 1885. One of Carver's lawyers questioned Buffalo Bill while all the responses were written out verbatim in longhand by a court stenographer. The questioning went on for hours, lasting until noon, when the hearing was adjourned and Bill headed to Meriden, Connecticut, to join his Wild West for a performance.[22]

After returning from Meriden that evening, Buffalo Bill picked up where he left off and continued to answer questions concerning his role in the stage dramas he acted in. Cody eventually testified that the name of the original show was changed from Carver and Cody's Wild West to Cody and Carver's Wild West because his name was more recognizable and would therefore be of greater benefit to the whole outfit. Bill also mentioned that the name soon became Buffalo Bill's Wild West for the very same reason.[23]

Cody went on to detail Doc Carver calling the enterprise the "Golden West" in many of his hometown Connecticut newspapers even though the two had not decided on that name. Buffalo Bill also testified he was the one who asked Carver to partner in his fledgling outdoor entertainment enterprise, which Carver accepted in early 1883. Prior to that time, Carver had no inkling of creating such a spectacle.[24]

On July 18, Cody's last scheduled day in Connecticut, Carver filed another suit against Bill and Salsbury for malicious prosecution, in which he claimed the two men had conspired to purposely try to ruin his business. Meanwhile, Cody's deposition continued during the sweltering hot and humid days of that Connecticut summer. By the last day of testimony, Bill was spent, both attorneys were spent, and the judge was irritated with little being accomplished. Cody eventually had his lawyers pony up a $52,000 bond just so he could get back on the road with his enterprise.[25]

Most newspapers in the New England states believed the lawsuits filed by both sides would never come to trial. And it is true, as most of the media outlets agreed, that if Carver would have compromised early on when the two shows started, "[both] could have gone through the country and made money."[26]

Through the whole ordeal, the two shows spent a great deal of time and money retaliating against each other, which cost both a great deal of business. Carver knew he would never get anything he was asking for and eventually settled for $10,000 in cash and Nate Salsbury to pay his remaining court costs. This action also allowed Carver to save some face after having to completely close his Wild West show due to the massive court costs he incurred. Because of the payout, Doc went on to tell people it was evidence Cody was a liar.[27]

Though Carver's Wild West went belly up, Doc went on to star in several other shows and circuses as a marksman and was reportedly quite the attraction. From 1889 to 1893, Carver toured around the continent with his "Wild America" outdoor show.[28]

Both Cody and Carver had similarities in appearance and in aspects of their performances, and equally fought for the rights to the Wild West title. There were marked and distinct differences between the competing showmen, however. Buffalo Bill, although he exaggerated at times to improve his stories, was the genuine article. He had grown up on the frontier, served as a military scout, and fought during the Indian Wars.

Bill was also friends with known gunfighters like Wild Bill Hickok and frontiersmen like Texas Jack Omohundro, both of whom backed up many of his claims. Cody received the Medal of Honor for his meritorious service during the Indian Wars and was a bison hunter during the construction of the Transcontinental Railroad. His reputation as an authentic frontiersman was well established before he ever stepped on stage.

Carver, on the other hand, shared none of these attributes. Most of Doc's early life remains shrouded in mystery, and many of his claims about his childhood have proven to be completely bogus. Carver had zero experience on the Great Plains or anywhere else on the western frontier. He focused much of his attention on his marksmanship and handling firearms, which he became quite good at. Carver then manufactured a pioneer persona to go with it. Most of the stories he shoveled were dubious at best and many were just outright fabrications.

The discrepancies between Bill and Doc do not end there either. As author and historian Sandra K. Sagala aptly put it, "The two former partners whose shows were so disparate in vision and concept makes [any] rivalry ludicrous."[29] Buffalo Bill designed his enterprise around his real experiences and hired a cast of authentic mountain men, Indians, and cowboys who were just as experienced on the frontier as he was. Cody was also well versed in the structure of the "blood and thunder" melodramas he

William Frank "Doc" Carver, circa 1925

performed onstage before ever stepping into the arena grounds. Carver had no experience with the above mentioned whatsoever.[30]

Unfortunately for Carver, many of his claims to the idea of the "Wild West" are totally without merit as well. Buffalo Bill created and launched the Old Glory Blowout outdoor spectacle in 1882. The Blowout contained many of the same themes Buffalo Bill's Wild West incorporated in its performances at least a year before Buffalo Bill ever approached Doc Carver to partner in a business venture. In fact, Bill's business manager Nate Salsbury had more of a claim to the title of the Wild West than Carver ever did.

Most believe that it was in fact Salsbury who initially conjured up the name Wild West. It has also been speculated over the years that when Nate approached Buffalo Bill in 1882 about starting an outdoor entertainment spectacle based on frontier life, Salsbury actually floated the Wild West name to Cody.[31] Whether this is actually true or not is a mystery, but the truth remains that Buffalo Bill had the concept before Carver ever came into the picture.

William Frank "Doc" Carver was not only a blowhard but also a straight-up thief. He stole the concept of the Wild West and incorporated the ideas into his own quickly cobbled together entertainment experience. What is perhaps even more egregious than his outright theft of intellectual property was his absolute lack of business acumen. Carver could have been a wealthy man had he only allowed Bill, and eventually Nate Salsbury, to run the show and agreed to Cody's name being first on the marquee. But, alas, his pride would not allow it.

In the early 1880s the Wild West traveling show concept was quickly becoming a lucrative one, and Buffalo Bill's enterprise was at the forefront of that innovation. It was almost a sure bet for any investor. But Carver's ego would not allow him to give ground on anything. Instead of great success, Carver cost himself his friendship and a partnership with Buffalo Bill, which eventually led to him being nothing more than a historical footnote.

CHAPTER 5

Superman before Superman

Faster than a speeding bullet, more powerful than a locomotive, able to leap tall buildings in a single bound! Yes, it's Superman—strange visitor from another planet who came to Earth with powers and abilities far beyond those of mortal men." These immortal words echoed from the mouths of radio announcers and narrators of cartoon reels on numerous episodic adventure tales introducing the world to Superman, Earth's mightiest hero.

The Last Son of Krypton became the joy and obsession of girls and boys all over the world (and of many adults for that matter). The creation of this hero eventually led to the superhero craze currently capturing Hollywood and most of today's moviegoing public. But before there was a Superman, a Spiderman, or even a team of Avengers there was Buffalo Bill Cody—the first American hero.

Now, imagine if you will, that Superman is a real being. Not just a fictional character popping out from the pages of a comic book saving the proverbial damsel in distress and foiling the deeds of evildoers. But an actual man, one with real-life experiences in battle, in braving new frontiers, and in creating allegiances with foreign peoples. Buffalo Bill Cody made this distinction during his early life, then built upon it throughout his entertainment career.

Granted, at the time of his first appearance on stage there were many true-to-life scouts, gunfighters, and military men who were trying their hand at show business. Yet none of these men seemed to have the drawing power and sustainable interest that Buffalo Bill maintained. It is, at times, hard to truly pinpoint what it was about William

THE BUFFALO BILL STORIES

A WEEKLY PUBLICATION   DEVOTED TO BORDER HISTORY

Issued Weekly. By subscription $2.50 per year. Entered as Second-class Matter at the N. Y. Post Office, by STREET & SMITH, 79-89 Seventh Ave., N. Y.

No. 320   NEW YORK, JUNE 29, 1907.   **Price, Five Cents**

With a startled cry, Buffalo Bill drew his horse back with a quick jerk as he saw before him that terrible skeleton figure with its shining eyes of fire.

Buffalo Bill in the Land of Spirits; or The Witch Hunters of the Hoodoo Mountains, *June 29, 1907*

Frederick Cody that made him such a star. By all accounts, he was not a great actor, and for some critics he was considered downright atrocious. The stories he appeared in were often quite formulaic and the usual sort of "blood and thunder" melodramas that proliferated across the American stage at the time.

Perhaps it was some combination of all these characteristics that eventually led to Bill's ultimate success, which culminated in the formation of his famous Wild West show. Most historians and biographers of Cody's life list affability as one of his most outstanding attributes. He was generally liked by audiences, and people were more than willing to plunk down cash to see him reenact a moment from his life on the frontier, or at least some heavily fictionalized version of it.

Bill, simply put, was a likable guy who women wanted and men wanted to be like. He had the "it" factor that is so often attributed to certain entertainers by Hollywood agents and producers looking to track down the next big star. The trait is often elusive and rarely found in the millions of Hollywood hopefuls who attempt a life of super-stardom. Most wash out or fail to reach the pinnacle, but occasionally one rises to the top, and William Frederick "Buffalo Bill" Cody was that man for the time in which he lived.

Stories of Buffalo Bill's heroic deeds, most of which were greatly embellished, graced the interiors of what were known at the time as "dime novels" or "nickel week-lies." Long before the comic book came into fashion, these inexpensive paperbound editions, typically a melodramatic romance or adventure story, were the cheap sought-after entertainment for children and adolescents of the day.

The heroes featured in the pages of these stories were not superhuman beings from far-off planets, or unsuspecting teenagers physically altered by some experiment gone wrong or a dip in a pool of toxic waste giving them godlike powers. Instead, many of the protagonists featured in these stories were often based on real people.

While many dime novels contained tales of the Western variety, others featured mysteries, detective stories, or titillating romances. Billy the Kid, Jesse James, Wild Bill Hickok, and of course Buffalo Bill had countless stories authored about them. Most of the stories were rooted in anything other than something resembling fact, but most people found them entertaining, easy to read, and readily available.

The phrase "dime novel" became a blanket term to describe any sort of formu-laic story containing lurid and sensationalistic adventure tales cheaply created and mass produced. For instance, the best of the stories from the nickel weeklies and dime

C813 I542 bus no. 310

THE BUFFALO BILL STORIES

A WEEKLY PUBLICATION — DEVOTED TO BORDER HISTORY

Issued Weekly. By subscription $2.50 per year. Entered as Second-class Matter at the N. Y. Post Office, by STREET & SMITH, 79-89 Seventh Ave., N. Y.

No. 310   NEW YORK, APRIL 20, 1907.   Price, Five Cents

The flash revealed a figure in ghostly white—the White Witch of the Niobrara. "Death! Death!" she cried, "to the one who opens the black secret of this canon."

Buffalo Bill Haunted; or The White Witch of Niobara, *April 20, 1907*

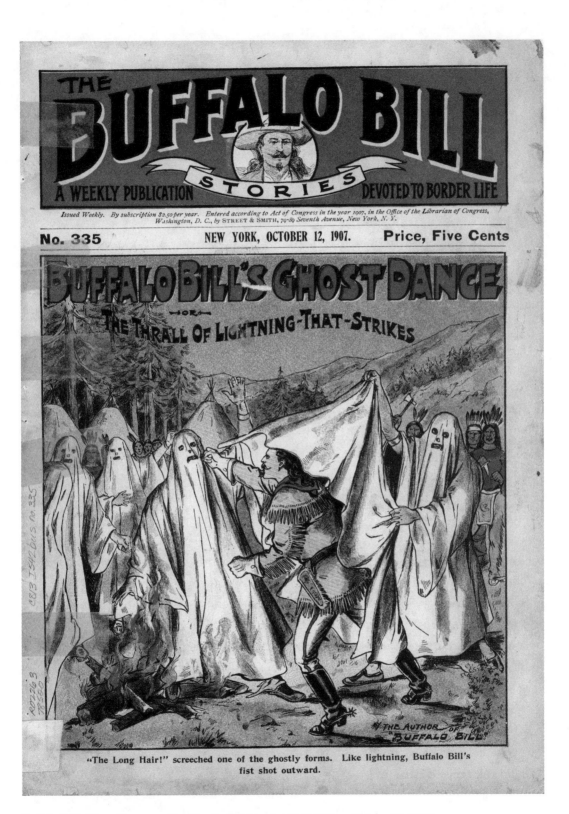

Buffalo Bill's Ghost Dance; or The Thrall of Lightening-That-Strikes, *October 12, 1907*

novels were compiled and reprinted into what were referred to as "thick-books" but also fell under the dime novel moniker.

Buffalo Bill first appeared in the pages of such fare in the early 1870s in stories first written by his compatriot Ned Buntline and then by his friend and press agent Prentiss Ingraham. Ingraham eventually wrote voluminous amounts of Buffalo Bill–related tales throughout the 1870s and 1880s. In fact, in 1900 Ingraham claimed to have written over six hundred novels. Nearly three hundred of those were Buffalo Bill stories. Along with the Buffalo Bill novels, Prentiss wrote the Buck Taylor series, Merle Monte series, and the Dick Doom series, respectively.[1]

Cody himself supposedly added to the total of the tales, claiming to have written at least thirteen of the novels himself. It is unclear if some of these novels were ghost-written or if they were collaborative efforts. It is interesting to note, however, that many of the novels were reprinted later under Prentiss Ingraham's name.[2] In fact, it is generally believed that Prentiss Ingraham ghostwrote most of the books Bill claimed to have penned. Cody did eventually gain a knack for the dime novel dialect and was adept at the "blood and thunder" style. So it is quite possible that he added to Ingraham's scripts and books.

Though these stories were often quite formulaic in their structure, they incorporated some elements that soon became features of traditional comic book storytelling familiar to twentieth-century audiences. Within the pages of these fantastical tales, Buffalo Bill would face off against imaginary beings with supernatural powers. In other stories, scientific experiments gone wrong would feature prominently, while yet others contained mysteries in the vein of *Scooby-Doo* television episodes. Comedy had its place and romance was always a theme in this form of fiction as well.

Today, many of these stories are nearly unreadable because of their slow-moving pace and verbose style that offers little to modern audiences. However, the dime novels and nickel weeklies from the nineteenth century laid the groundwork for what has currently become one of the most important and lucrative categories in the publishing industry, comic books.

Buffalo Bill was easily the most popular of all the dime novel heroes. Starring as the hero in the most popular stage plays as well as having an authentic background as a frontiersman led to Bill being an instant success among the novel-reading public. But there were times when Cody attempted to distance himself from the dime novels that helped build this reputation.

C813 I542 bus no. 330

THE BUFFALO BILL STORIES

A WEEKLY PUBLICATION — DEVOTED TO BORDER LIFE

Issued Weekly. By subscription $2.50 per year. Entered as Second-class Matter at the N. Y. Post Office, by STREET & SMITH, 79-89 Seventh Ave., N. Y.

No. 330   NEW YORK, SEPTEMBER 7, 1907.   **Price, Five Cents**

BUFFALO BILL'S OUTLAW TRAIL
~OR~
THE MYSTERY OF THE TETON BASIN

BY THE AUTHOR OF "BUFFALO BILL"

The outlaws cheered wildly as the baloon lifted Buffalo Bill skyward.

Buffalo Bill's Outlaw Trail; or The Mystery of the Teton Basin, *September 7, 1907*

For fear of gaining a reputation as a dime novel scout, Bill did not want to be associated too closely with these fanciful stories. Because of this connection, Cody was sometimes seen as a caricature of the man he truly was. In 1885, when questioned by some newspaper men, Cody recoiled from the idea that one of his closest confidants and the man who helped launch his career, Ned Buntline, was nothing more than a dime novel author.[3]

Another reason why Bill desired to distance himself from the dime novels was because of his wish to secure status among the country's cultural elite. Many of the people who consumed this lurid literature were working-class types. These novels were considered a form of entertainment for those who could not afford to plunk down the cash to purchase tickets for a stage play but still wanted to experience the thrill of Buffalo Bill's prairie tales.[4]

More importantly was the fact that Buffalo Bill desperately desired to be associated with upward mobility and the elite in cities like New York. He felt that to achieve approval in those circles he needed to disassociate himself from the commoners, including their reading material. Though he never forgot his roots and experiences on the Great Plains, Cody became quite ambivalent toward the hundreds of dime novels in which he appeared.[5]

In fact, Bill even became quite self-deprecating toward the plays and tales he starred in, telling reporters that Ned Buntline wrote *The Scouts of the Prairie* in an afternoon. He said he was so nervous when he went onstage that he forgot all his lines, and only by the grace of Buntline, who was on stage with him, was he able to mutter his way to the finish of the production. Bill portrayed himself as even more of a nonprofessional, saying, "I didn't try to act. I did what I used to do on the prairie, not what I thought some other fellow might have done if he felt that way."[6]

Though Cody mocked his own appearance in the plays and novels he appeared in, he continued to show up in their pages and would do so for over three decades, almost up until his death in 1917. Through those years there were multiple publishers who tried to muscle in on the popularity of the dime novel, but one stands out above the other competing companies, Beadle's.

Two brothers, Erastus and Irwin Beadle, released the first dime novel through the enterprise known as Irwin P. Beadle & Co. in 1860. The first book in the Beadle's library was *Malaeska, the Indian Wife of the White Hunter*, by Ann S. Stephens. This novel was a reprint of Stephens's earlier serial, which originally appeared in installments in

THE BUFFALO BILL

STORIES

A WEEKLY PUBLICATION — DEVOTED TO BORDER HISTORY

Issued Weekly. By subscription $2.50 per year. Entered as Second-class Matter at the N. Y. Post Office, by STREET & SMITH, 79-89 Seventh Ave., N. Y.

No. 245   NEW YORK, JANUARY 20, 1906.   Price, Five Cents

BUFFALO BILL'S LOST QUARRY
OR FOLLOWING A COLD TRAIL

BY THE AUTHOR OF "BUFFALO BILL"

Buffalo Bill drew his bowie-knife and stabbed at the animal's neck, to force it to swerve out of the herd and release him from his deadly peril.

Buffalo Bill's Lost Quarry; or Following a Cold Trail, *January 20, 1906*

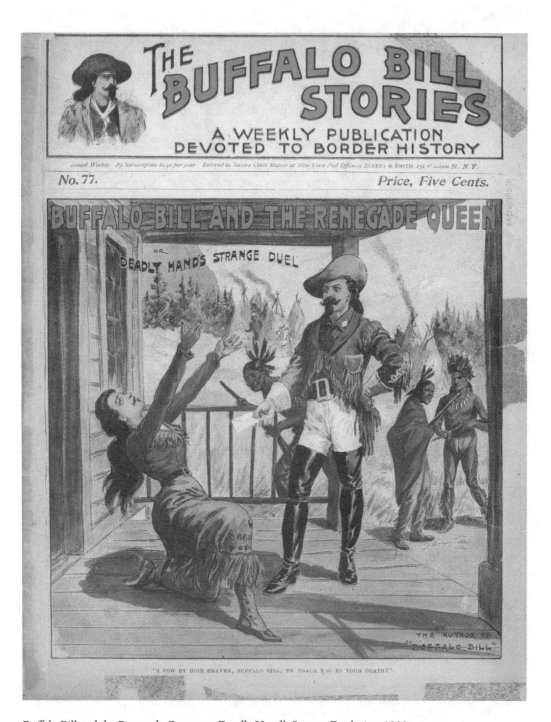

Buffalo Bill and the Renegade Queen; or Deadly Hand's Strange Duel, *circa 1902*

the magazine *Ladies Companion*. After its initial success the company merged with another publisher and soon became known as Beadle & Adams.[7]

These offerings from Beadle's, of course, cost one thin dime when they were first printed. When the genre began to proliferate, prices ranged anywhere from five to fifteen cents. Yet all these publications were universally known as dime novels. Brandeis Special Collections at Brandeis University, which contains thousands of dime novels, describes the genre thusly: "[T]he dime novel exploited cheap printing, newly efficient distribution, and a broader reading [for a] public hungry for sensational yarns involving detectives, cowboys, and romantic heroines."[8] Dime novels truly became a catchall for anything deemed "low brow" by critics from the upper crust of society. Even so, they were very popular, and Buffalo Bill capitalized on them.

The first twenty-eight volumes in the Beadle's library were published without a cover illustration and were usually enfolded in a salmon-colored wrapping paper. As competitors arose, however, the need for cover illustrations became paramount. The art employed was usually eye catching, and in many ways was more intriguing and exhilarating than the story contained in the novels themselves. This outlandish art also paved the way for the familiar comic book–style illustrations popular with modern audiences.[9]

As the lively and entertaining covers for these publications improved, Beadle's and its competitors republished many of their former stories with different cover art in order to ignite new interest in old titles. Publishers would often reprint two or more stories with similar themes in what was referred to as a "giant issue."

These business practices are quite common and used frequently in today's comic book industry. Publishers, to maximize profits from a special edition or first issues of a title, reprint these titles with a "variant" or "alternate" cover. Interestingly, the practice of creating cover art to catch the eye stretched beyond comic books and became a staple of video rental stores across the country. Many VHS tapes and later DVDs used unique cover art to entice people to rent and purchase videos that often had little if anything to do with the content contained on the tapes and discs. Most of these productions were in the action and horror genres, cheaply made and quickly produced. Eye-catching covers also came into vogue with paperback novels and continue to be used as an effective sales tool today.

The first comic book marketed with a variant cover was the 1986 first issue of *The Man of Steel* (one of many titles featuring Superman), which featured two different

THE BUFFALO BILL STORIES

A WEEKLY PUBLICATION — DEVOTED TO BORDER HISTORY

Issued Weekly. By subscription $2.50 per year. Entered as Second-class Matter at the N. Y. Post Office, by STREET & SMITH, *79-89 Seventh Ave., N. Y.*

No. 316   NEW YORK, JUNE 1, 1907.   **Price, Five Cents**

"You dance to your death with me now," cried the gruesome figure, seizing the scout and whirling him round. It was the strangely-attired man known as The Red Death.

Buffalo Bill's Dance with Death; or Peril on the Golconda Gold Trail, *June 1, 1907*

covers with unique art produced by writer and artist John Byrne.[10] The practice of variant covers became more pronounced during the early 1990s during a time for comics that has become known as the "speculators boom." This boom took place when more collectors became interested in the storage and preservation of their comic books with the goal of future financial gain rather than reading the comics themselves.

To capitalize on the speculative market, publishers like DC, Marvel, and Image Comics relaunched some of their most popular titles, starting them over at issue one even though in some cases these titles had already climbed into the hundreds of issues. Then the covers of these relaunched titles received variants. These publishing houses also created embossed covers, holographic covers, and 3-D covers, and placed trading cards and stickers in polybags with special anniversary books—all to make a quick buck off ravenous collectors who were searching for the next rare item to add to their hoard.

Around this time, publishers also began collecting stories with a beginning and ending story arc into one volume. This publication is what has been popularly referred to as the "graphic novel," which is a trade paperback or a collected story. This practice continues today and remains quite popular.

What was the result of all this relaunching, trade paperbacks, and cover manipulation? It spawned the production of comic books with barely coherent stories, garbage art, and the near bankruptcy of the entire comic industry. Only the creative rethinking of the comic format, focus on quality books over quantity, and the eventual creation of movies based on comic characters with high-quality production values saved the industry from total ruin.

What is so interesting about the current comic book market is how similar it is to the dime novel industry of Buffalo Bill's time. Cody graced the pages of hundreds of volumes. Nearly all the top publishers wanted to feature him or a cheap imitation of him in their books. Those novels featuring Buffalo Bill were often reprinted with variant covers or with two or more of the stories combined into one volume. Often, the combined stories were slightly rewritten to try to tie the stories together.[11]

Although he had a spot in Beadles & Adams publications, Buffalo Bill, as a superhero protagonist, was featured mostly in Street & Smith novels. Founded in 1855 by Francis Scott Street and Francis Shubal Smith, Street & Smith published dime novels, pulp fiction magazines, and eventually comic books. The company also covered sports quite extensively in their nonfiction division.

LESTER-SCOTT-

THE BUFFALO BILL STORIES

A WEEKLY PUBLICATION   DEVOTED TO BORDER HISTORY

Issued Weekly. By subscription $2.50 per year. Entered as Second-class Matter at the N. Y. Post Office, by STREET & SMITH, 79-89 Seventh Ave., N. Y.

No. 244   NEW YORK, JANUARY 13, 1906.   **Price Five Cents**

BUFFALO BILL ON A TREASURE HUNT

or THE SECRET HOARD OF THE YAQUIS

BY THE AUTHOR OF "BUFFALO BILL"

Before Buffalo Bill could draw his revolver, the Yaqui grappled with him. Then began a
fearful struggle for life on the brink of that deadly chasm.

Buffalo Bill on a Treasure Hunt; or The Secret Hoard of the Yaquis, *January 13, 1906*

Buffalo Bill and the Rope Wizard, *February 13, 1909*

Cody, as a character, was featured in multiple publications from Street & Smith including *Buffalo Bill Stories* with 591 issues from 1902 to 1915, *Buffalo Bill Border Stories* with 211 issues from 1917 to 1925, *New Buffalo Bill Weekly* with 356 issues from 1912 to 1919, and eventually *New Buffalo Bill Weekly*, which morphed into the pulp magazine *Western Story Magazine* and ran from 1919 to 1949, selling over half a million copies per issue![12] Many of these volumes went into publication after Buffalo Bill died in 1917, proving his popularity and staying power.

Many of the images that eventually played out in live action during Buffalo Bill's Wild West appeared on the covers of the dime novels and nickel weeklies and were described in detail within their pages. Cody fighting to the death with Yellow Hair, hunting bison, charging headlong into a burning homestead, and riding on his mighty steed to shoot glass balls out of the air were all part of the dime novels in which he appeared.[13]

Cody even reprinted some of the material from *Beadle's Weekly* dime novels into the souvenir programs for his Wild West show. This reprinted material normally included romanticized poetry alongside some of his true exploits.[14] The combination of the two helped build the image of the undaunted Buffalo Bill who could do anything and was the king of the wild frontier.

Not only were Buffalo Bill's exploits in fiction exciting and entertaining, they also provided a window into the American consciousness. These stories told the tales of a closing frontier and a changing American West. They gave readers a glimpse at a bygone era, the vanishing frontier that people longed for and many children dreamed about. These pieces of fiction allowed people to experience the Wild West vicariously through a cheap form of literature. And all these stories portrayed the settling of the West in a romantic light, giving a happy ending to numerous narratives.[15]

The dime novels, much like comic books of today, provided escapist stories allowing readers to lose themselves for a short time. In a world that was changing with the Civil War quickly becoming a memory and the western frontier fading, the dime novel allowed people to forget the hardships of the past and to take a moment for a bit of frivolity. These novels were a chance for people to escape the doldrums and trappings of everyday life and go on an adventure with the heroes they wished existed in their own lives.

The dime novel's time, however, eventually came to an end. In 1896, the juvenile magazine *Argosy* eventually morphed into a fiction magazine for adults and

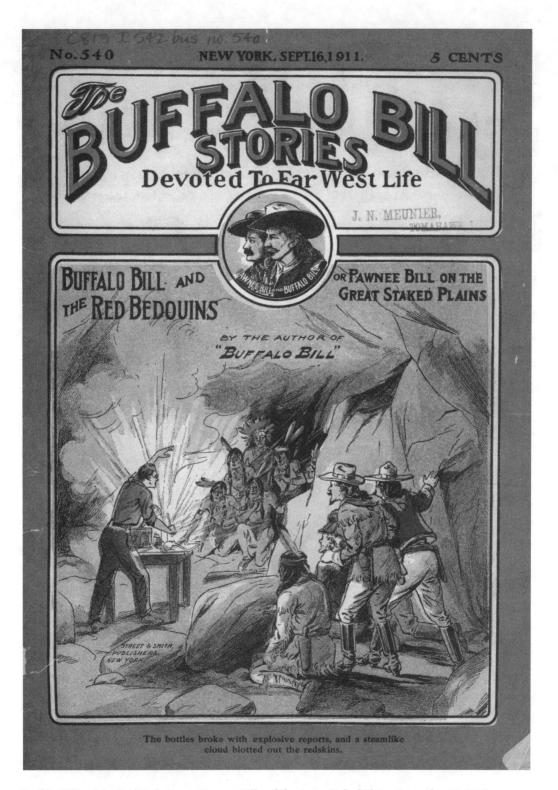

Buffalo Bill and the Red Bedouins or Pawnee Bill and the Great Staked Plains, *September 16, 1911.*

is considered the first of the pulp magazines. Accompanying the change from the dime novel format to the pulp magazine was the ability for publishers to create magazines at a greater rate with new high-speed printing techniques and cheap pulp paper.[16] The cheap stock and the new publication techniques allowed publishers to lower prices and churn out a greater number of stories for the public to consume.

Although actual "dime" novels were replaced by the even cheaper pulp magazines, the term dime novel remained in use for quite some time. In fact, the term was so recognized by the public that in the 1940s the popular pulp magazine *Western Dime Novels* featured the term prominently on its cover.[17]

Covering the death of the dime novel, Martyn Lyons wrote in his volume, *Books: A Living History*, "In 1910, Street and Smith converted two of their nickel weeklies, *New Tip Top Weekly* and *Top Notch Magazine*, into pulps; in 1915, Nick Carter Stories, itself a replacement for the *New Nick Carter Weekly*, became *Detective Story Magazine*, and in 1919, *New Buffalo Bill Weekly* became *Western Story Magazine*."[18]

By 1926 Street & Smith purchased the rights to the last of the continuously published dime novels. The most notable of them were *Secret Service*, *Pluck and Luck*, *Fame and Fortune*, and *Wild West Weekly*. Street & Smith converted these publications into pulp magazines the following year, which effectively ended the era of the dime novel.[19]

Though the dime novel died in the late 1920s, the character of Buffalo Bill lived on through the pulp magazines. And when the pulps eventually lost their luster, Bill marched on in popular publications like comic strips in daily newspapers and comic books on newsstands. Finding his way out of the funny papers and onto the pages of modern comic books cemented Buffalo Bill's place among the superheroes who were just being born and becoming icons to countless children in America.

Bill first appeared in what is an officially recognized comic book in the first 1933 issue of *Men of Daring*.[20] Cody is considered a golden-age-of-comics character, who consistently appeared in comic books throughout the 1930s and into the 1950s. Bill would go on to star in his own series, titled *Buffalo Bill*, which ran for fifty-two issues and would also appear in comics ranging from famous titles like *Wonder Woman* and *Action Comics* to *Popeye* and *Uncle Scrooge*.

Buffalo Bill's Heathen Pard; or Lung Hi on the Warpath, *December 16, 1905*

As a character, and as of this writing, Buffalo Bill last appeared in *Calamity Jane: The Calamitous Life of Martha Jane Cannary*, a graphic novel published by Top Shelf Comics in 2017.[21] Dime novels, pulp magazines, and comic books are additional proof that Buffalo Bill lives on in popular culture and remains at the forefront of the American consciousness.

CHAPTER 6
An Unlikely Cast of Characters

With the establishment of Buffalo Bill's Wild West, Cody began to compile an all-star cast for his show. Unlike other showmen in the business, however, Bill did not choose all of his cast from the rank and file of stage actors and circus performers. Instead he often hired people who had real-life experience on the frontier but also had little to no knowledge of the performing arts. Bill employed these men and women because he felt they gave his enterprise authenticity. He saw the Wild West as a historic reenactment, not a circus spectacle. Bill wanted real frontiersmen to represent that ideal.

Cody started by hiring John Young Nelson, who became an integral part of the show. Better known as "Old Man Nelson," John Young originally supported himself as a trapper and scout and was married to a Brulé Sioux woman named Jenny Yellow Elk Woman. The two had several children before he signed on with Cody's outfit. Their children became performers in the Wild West as well.[1]

Nelson initially was an interpreter for the numerous Sioux Indians in the show. His most important contribution to the enterprise, however, was as the driver of the Deadwood Stagecoach.[2] The stagecoach rode out at the beginning of nearly every Wild West show performance. Almost as popular as Buffalo Bill himself, the Deadwood Stagecoach became synonymous with the Wild West performances.

Along with Nelson, Bill soon employed a man named William Levi "Buck" Taylor. An exceptional horseman who could leap from the backs of racing steeds and rope anything that moved, Taylor was quickly nicknamed "King of the Cowboys" because

A member of the cast of Buffalo Bill's Wild West, possibly John Y. Nelson, stands tied to a tall, wooden stake during a performance of the show at Earl's Court in England, circa 1887.

Miss Annie Oakley, "Little Sure Shot," Buffalo Bill's Wild West. Photo by Elliott & Fry, circa 1885.

of this advanced skill with horseflesh. Taylor was also part of the original cast of the Wild West but had also worked for Cody as a ranch hand in Nebraska.[3] Bill gave Buck a chance to earn a living working for the Wild West and afforded him the opportunity to be one of its earliest stars. Taylor had the fitness for the job he was given and proved to be a fan favorite.

Bill's greatest stroke of luck, however, came when he acquired the services of the woman who would go on to be a fixture in the Wild West and in the hearts of Americans everywhere, Annie Oakley. Along with her husband, Frank Butler, and under the direction and management of Nate Salsbury, Oakley was hired as a performer for the Wild West in 1885.[4]

Phoebe Ann Moses (sometimes referred to as Mosey) was born in 1860 near Greenville, Ohio. As she told it, Annie learned to shoot at the age of eight and became an accomplished markswoman and hunter by the time she was a teenager. She supplied game for locals and businesses in and around Greenville because her family was poor. At the age of fifteen, Annie outdid her future husband, Frank Butler, an accomplished shooter in his own right, in a shooting contest in Cincinnati before a large crowd of onlookers. The two married in 1876 and in 1882 began performing marksmanship shows together.[5]

Annie quickly concocted the stage name of Oakley, derived from the city neighborhood in which she and Frank lived in Ohio. Their act was popular from the onset, and her diminutive size (five feet, two inches) and pretty face, combined with her lethal accuracy and gentle demeanor, made her an instant attraction. Annie usually began her routine by blowing out candles with bullets, snuffing out cigarettes from her husband's mouth, and blasting corks off bottles. One of her more famous routines was shooting holes in playing cards held by Frank or another assistant.[6]

Acting as her manager, Frank eventually finagled a lucrative deal with Buffalo Bill's Wild West. Annie and Frank would remain with the troupe through multiple tours of Europe and the United States until they eventually left the show in 1901 to pursue their own interests.[7]

A large part of Annie's popularity was undoubtedly due to her being a woman and possessing the marksman skills of a backwoodsman. But Annie was much more than a novelty. She had a charisma that few could claim. People were drawn to her, much like they were drawn to Buffalo Bill. She was friendly with the crowds, especially

Walks-Under-the-Ground and Kishvardi Makharadze, a Russian Georgian Cossack, pose in Buffalo Bill's Wild West, circa 1890.

spectators' children. Her attire was as reserved as her stage persona, which made her immediately relatable and likable.

When Annie toured with the Wild West overseas, her performances were well regarded. Legend has it that while Oakley was in Europe on tour with the Wild West, she shot the ashes off a cigarette held by Kaiser Wilhelm II upon his request.[8] In 1894, when Thomas Edison created the film camera, one of the earliest subjects he thought to record was Buffalo Bill's Wild West. Both Annie and Frank performed in the film, with Annie shooting glass balls tossed by Frank. Interestingly, the movie is believed to be only the eleventh motion picture ever produced.[9]

With Oakley's stage presence and ability to draw large crowds wherever she went, Buffalo Bill paid her like the star she was. In fact, Bill paid most of his female performers just as well as his male stars. Referring to this subject, Bill was quoted as saying, "What we want to do is give women even more liberty than they have. Let them do any kind of work they see fit, and if they do it as well as men, give them the same pay."[10]

Annie Oakley was given the nickname of "Little Sure Shot" by another superstar Bill was fortunate enough to wrangle into the Wild West show, Sioux chief Sitting Bull. The great chief and medicine man of the Sioux tribe dubbed Annie Watanya Cicilla, commonly translated as "Little Sure Shot" but literally meaning "Little Person Who Does Good Things." He gave her this title after seeing her perform with her husband on tour. Coincidentally, Sitting Bull also joined Buffalo Bill's Wild West in 1885, the same year as Annie.[11]

Sitting Bull became so smitten with Annie when he first saw her perform that he offered to pay her $65 for her photo. He is also reported to have told Annie he wanted to adopt her on multiple occasions. After dealing with the old man's obsession, the two became good friends during their time with the Wild West.[12]

Although Sitting Bull achieved great acclaim for his performances in Buffalo Bill's Wild West, he was almost not a part of the show at all. In May 1885 Cody attempted to recruit Sitting Bull, but Major James McLaughlin, the agent in charge of Fort Randall where Sitting Bull was living, rejected Bill's attempt to hire him. Over the years many circuses and religious organizations had attempted to employ Sitting Bull before Cody ever approached the idea. McLaughlin rejected each of them, stating he wanted Sitting Bull and his compatriots to adjust to agricultural life.[13]

Though he was initially rebuffed, Bill would not be deterred. His hunt for Sitting Bull mirrored many of his hunts for bison on the Great Plains—Buffalo Bill simply would not be denied while pursuing his prey. To attract Sitting Bull, Cody encouraged several high society individuals to write letters of recommendation for the chief's inclusion in the Wild West show, including former foes of Sitting Bull's like General William Tecumseh Sherman and Colonel Eugene Asa Carr.[14]

Finally relenting to the constant badgering by Buffalo Bill, McLaughlin agreed to allow Sitting Bull to join the Wild West along with some of his fellow tribesmen. On June 6, 1885, Arizona John Burke made the arrangements to have Sitting Bull sign a contract that would pay him $50 a week, a $125 signing bonus, and two weeks' salary in advance. The five other Indians who accompanied him received $25 per week in pay. It is interesting to note that these salaries were comparable to the contracts of any of the other performers employed in the Wild West show. In addition to his weekly salary and bonuses, Sitting Bull had a clause written into his contract allowing him to sell autographs and his portrait while keeping all the proceeds.[15]

After securing this highly lucrative deal, both Burke and Sitting Bull boarded a train headed to Buffalo, New York, where they were met by a throng of eager and cheering fans. After navigating the crowd, Sitting Bull joined the Wild West troupe already on tour. He was then immediately thrust into a reenactment.[16] After his first acting turn, the revered medicine man became a star attraction in the enterprise and packed performance grounds with spectators who wanted nothing more than to get a glimpse of the famous chief.[17]

Buffalo Bill and Sitting Bull also became friends during the time they shared together in the Wild West show. Apparently, at one point during Sitting Bull's time in the show, he gave Buffalo Bill a bear claw necklace, signifying the bond between them.[18] At the close of the performing season in 1885, Sitting Bull returned to his home at the Standing Rock Reservation in Dakota Territory. He gave his reasons for leaving by saying, "The wigwam is a better place for the red man. [I am] sick of the houses and noises and the multitudes of men." On the night of his last performance, Sitting Bull went to his beloved Little Sure Shot and presented Annie with a quiver of the finest arrows, beaded moccasins, and a feathered headdress.[19]

After giving Annie the kingly gifts, Sitting Bull and she stood together for a moment then walked out of the tent into the rainy night. Looking off into the night sky, Sitting Bull told Annie, "It will be a cold winter." After this somewhat intimate moment, the two shared a meal in the cook tent with the rest of the Wild West performers.[20]

Sitting Bull and Buffalo Bill, taken by W. Notman, copyright David Francis Barry, 1885

Before the great medicine man returned to the reservation, however, Buffalo Bill took Sitting Bull aside and presented him with a western-style hat and the trained show horse Sitting Bull had ridden for the four months he was with the Wild West. Being a show pony, the horse was said to have been trained to "dance" when it heard gunshots. During these performances the steed would pick up its hooves and begin clip-clopping to the rhythm of the bullets being fired.[21]

Sitting Bull cherished both the hat and the horse, taking the gifts with him when he returned to his home on the Standing Rock Reservation. Some historians believe that when Sitting Bull was killed outside his home on December 15, 1890, during a failed attempt to arrest him by Lakota reservation policemen, the beloved horse Cody gave him began to dance when the bullets flew between the officers and Sitting Bull's supporters. According to historian and author Deanne Stillman, the horse arched his neck and pranced in a circle. He bowed and then stood up and shook his long mane, pawed the ground, and reared up and leaped into the air. He cantered around and around in a circle, stopped, and backed up, and then cantered some more.[22]

The horse was eventually used as a mount by one of the reservation policemen, who rode the animal to summon reinforcements to Sitting Bull's cabin. After notifying the reinforcements, the rider began to spread the word of Sitting Bull's death throughout the reservation. Following the assassination of the Lakota leader, the horse was returned to his widows. When Buffalo Bill learned of the travesty, he offered to pay the women for the horse, which they accepted. Later in 1893, outside the Columbian Exposition in Chicago, the horse was ridden in a parade of Buffalo Bill's Wild West and draped in an American flag in honor of Sitting Bull.[23]

Another integral performer in Buffalo Bill's Wild West was Lewis H. "Johnny" Baker. Johnny has often been referred to as Buffalo Bill's foster son. Following the death of his biological son, Kit Carson Cody, at the age of five in 1876, Bill was left with a void in his life and in his heart. Cody warmed to young Johnny Baker when he was only seven years old. Although his parents never allowed Cody to officially adopt him, Johnny nevertheless traveled, worked, and studied with Buffalo Bill for most of his life. Cody taught Johnny how to shoot and quickly transformed the young boy into an expert marksman. Baker became a sharpshooting star of the Wild West show, and later was manager and worldwide show booker for the enterprise until Cody's death in 1917.[24]

Johnny Baker poses on horseback with a pistol pointed up in the air, circa 1890.

Johnny Baker was born in western Nebraska at O'Fallon's Bluffs near the South Platte River, around 1870. His father was Lew Baker, the owner of Lew Baker O'Fallon's Bluff Ranch, considered by many to be a landmark on the Overland Trail. Young Johnny grew up during a time when hostile Sioux tribes were still roaming the range along Nebraska's Great Plains.[25] It is reported Johnny grew up admiring the cowboys working on the ranch and longed to join them in their occupation.[26]

When the railroad supplanted stagecoach lines, the use of the Overland Trail became obsolete. Reading the writing on the wall, Lew Baker moved his family to the cowboy town of North Platte. Lew built a home that became a house of hospitality where he hosted many old-time cowboys who had worked for him during his days running the Bluff Ranch. In North Platte, Johnny began working extensively for Buffalo Bill, whose homestead and extensive horse and cattle ranches were in the area. It is here that Cody took Johnny under his wing and Baker became recognized as "Buffalo Bill's boy."[27]

During the winter Baker occasionally went to school. However, when Cody established Buffalo Bill's Wild West in 1883, it was a foregone conclusion that Johnny Baker would be involved in the enterprise. With his shooting, riding, and lassoing skills, it was said Baker could "break every man in the outfit." Johnny soon became known as "The Cow-Boy Kid."[28] Baker's shooting style was much like sharpshooter Captain Adam Henry Bogardus, who had toured with Buffalo Bill's Wild West in 1883.

Baker loved Buffalo Bill and saw him as a father figure. After Bill's death, Johnny established the Buffalo Bill Memorial Museum in 1921. Johnny filled the museum with artifacts, documents, and photographs that he had accumulated over thirty-five years as Buffalo Bill's unofficial foster son. Interestingly, Baker was the same age that Cody's son, Kit, would have been had he not died of scarlet fever. Today the Buffalo Bill Museum remains near William Cody's grave site, on Lookout Mountain near the town of Golden, Colorado. The museum continues to further Baker's purpose of educating visitors about the life and times of Buffalo Bill.[29]

Somehow, this odd assortment of personalities helped make Buffalo Bill's Wild West the sensation it quickly became. Many of them did not know one another when they entered the enterprise, but several had one trait in common. Most of the Wild

Buffalo Bill Cody at his home at Scout's Rest Ranch in North Platte, Nebraska, circa 1887

Buffalo Bill's Wild West, including Annie Oakley and Buffalo Bill, circa 1885.

West troupe were frontiersmen and women who had braved the wilderness and helped tame the West. Many were hardscrabble pioneers who decided to give acting a try—and in doing so, helped create one of the most memorable enterprises in entertainment history.

CHAPTER 7
Unstable Ground

Though Buffalo Bill would eventually achieve international superstardom, he would have his troubles along the way. As Cody was quickly building his reputation as an actor and showman with the launch of his Wild West enterprise in 1883, he soon suffered a great deal of financial distress. In joining forces with Nate Salsbury, Cody found a manager who had the experience, intelligence, and ability to make Buffalo Bill's Wild West a financial success. But unforeseen circumstances in late 1884 nearly led to the bankruptcy of the entire outfit, and if not for a fortuitous introduction to a wealthy young Englishman, Buffalo Bill's Wild West may never have become the legendary enterprise it did.

In October 1884, during the halcyon days of America's Gilded Age, a wealthy young Englishman named Evelyn Booth ventured to the United States to sample all that the burgeoning country had to offer. As the young sportsman traveled from New York to Chicago to Arkansas and finally to New Orleans, he tumbled into his greatest adventure—a shooting match with Buffalo Bill Cody before a crowd of three thousand spectators. Although he failed to bag a shooting trophy, the chance encounter with the king of American showmen gave Booth an opportunity to partner in one of the most profitable and renowned Western enterprises ever.

Born in 1860 to well-to-do English parents in Dublin, Ireland, Evelyn Thomas Barton Booth attended Trinity College in Cambridge, England. Evelyn was born into a long line of baronets in the British aristocracy. The baronetcy is a hereditary title awarded by the British Crown. The Booths were among the first eighteen families

Portrait of Evelyn Booth, 1884

raised to the baronetage when the Order of Baronets was first instituted by James I in 1611 as a means of raising money for the monarchy. All baronets and baronetesses receive the title of Sir or Lady much like an individual who has been knighted, but they are a much higher rank then a traditional knight.[1]

The Booths have been historically aristocratic with their family line including Sir Felix Booth, a wealthy gin distiller,[2] and Sir Alfred Allen Booth, who was the former chairman of the Cunard Steamship Company.[3] The Booth family line also includes numerous generous philanthropists, members of parliament, clergy, and current television and film producers. Since the inception of the baronetcy in 1611, there have been fifteen Booth family baronets with the lineage surviving well into the twenty-first century.[4]

Two years after graduating from Trinity College, Evelyn Booth and two companions set sail for America on the steamship RMS *Oregon*, a Cunard Line steamship, which docked in Sandy Hook, New Jersey, on November 2, 1884. Once in the United States, Booth caroused in infamous brothels, frequented gambling houses, and obtained front-row seats at a John L. Sullivan heavyweight boxing title fight. Sullivan is widely considered the first gloved heavyweight champion of the world.[5]

Much like Booth, his traveling companions Reginald Beaumont Heygate and Dr. John Percival Frizzle were also members of the English upper class. At a time when their less adventurous friends were embarking on safe but clichéd grand tours of the European capitals, this group of young friends took a "buddy trip" from England to America. These three young men would most likely be described today as "frat boys" or "bros," but were referred to as "sportsmen" during this period.[6]

After traveling with his friends on their trip around America, Reginald Heygate would go on to live a rather uneventful life. Born in 1857 in London, England, to Constance M. and William Unwin Heygate, a magistrate for the county of Hertfordshire, England, Reginald graduated from Cambridge University with a BA in 1880 and an MA in 1883. He eventually worked as an assistant private secretary to Sir William Harcourt in 1886 but died unmarried in 1903. His cause of death could not be found on any historical record.[7]

Dr. John Percival Frizzle, on the other hand, was born in Belfast, Ireland, in 1862. Frizzle, after returning to the UK in 1885, would eventually immigrate to the United States in 1889. He married Sarah "Sadie" W. Rhodes in 1894. After the marriage ended, Frizzle remarried in 1905 to Lena Frances Parker and the couple had twin girls: Lena

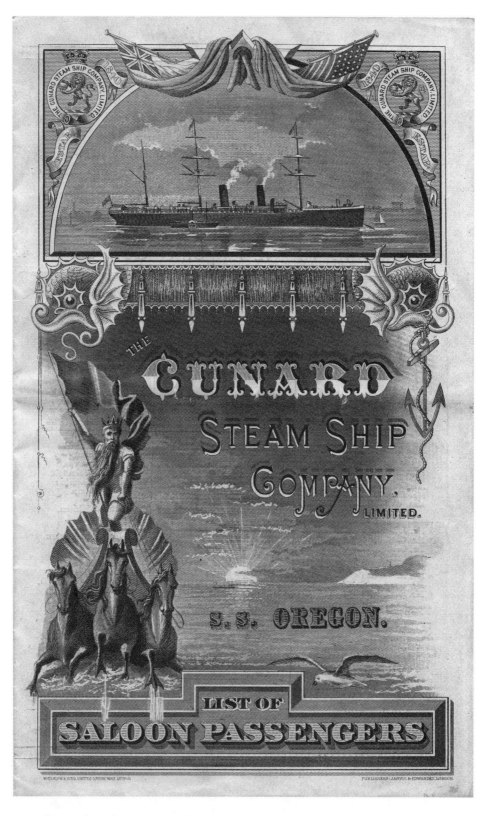

Cunard Steamship Saloon Passenger List, 1884

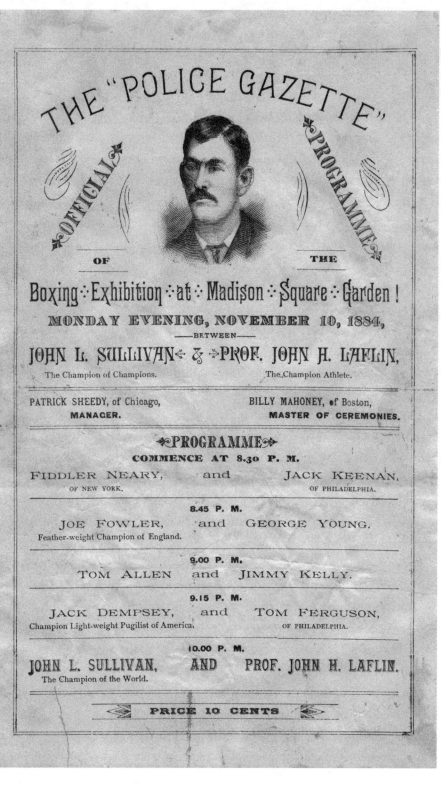

The Police Gazette, *boxing exhibition at Madison Square Garden, official program, 1885*

Parker Frizzle and Frances Percival Frizzle. The family lived in northern California, in Siskiyou County. As far as what type of doctor Frizzle was, it is hard to determine, but he did have a fascination for taxidermy.[8]

Dr. Frizzle also spent time in British Columbia's Klondike and Yukon Territory. Later in life John would gain some notoriety for organizing multiple attempts to track a mastodon he believed to be living in the Alaskan wilderness. Unfortunately for Frizzle, his expeditions bore no fruit and he was considered a bit of a crackpot toward the end of his life.[9]

In 1884, however, these three young scoundrels, after disembarking in New Jersey, would also be joined by the most famous horse jockey of the day, Frederick James Archer. A champion horseman, Archer was one of the most renowned Englishmen in sporting circles. Born in 1857 he became a horse jockey by the age of fifteen, and during the late nineteenth century he rose to prominence as England's most celebrated competitive rider. During his short but storied career, Archer won the Epsom Derby five times and won twenty-one other classic races.[10] In today's terms Archer would be the equivalent of a jockey who has ridden multiple Triple Crown winners.

A close friend of Evelyn Booth's, Fred Archer arrived in America in December 1884.[11] He quickly joined Booth and his companions while they caroused throughout the country. Although he seemed to have everything, Archer committed suicide only two short years later, in 1886. It is reported that his death, from a self-inflicted gunshot wound, was brought on by several factors: massive weight loss stemming from his constant binge dieting to maintain his weight as a jockey, a bout with a fever, and severe depression from the loss of his wife, Nellie Rose Dawson, who died of scarlet fever in late 1884.[12]

Before the death of Nellie Rose, however, Archer and his companions enjoyed the denizens of brothels all over the United States. As avid hunters, these young men also wanted to make their way to Colorado in hopes of killing a grizzly bear, but for unsubstantiated reasons they were unable to make their way to the Rocky Mountain state. So they decided to take in the sights of one of the country's most unique cities, New Orleans.

While in the Crescent City, Booth and his companions partook in one of the most popular and notorious games of chance of the day, faro. This game would weigh heavily in the future dealings of the men, and eventually led to Booth and Buffalo Bill becoming connected. This turned out to be a truly fortuitous circumstance that

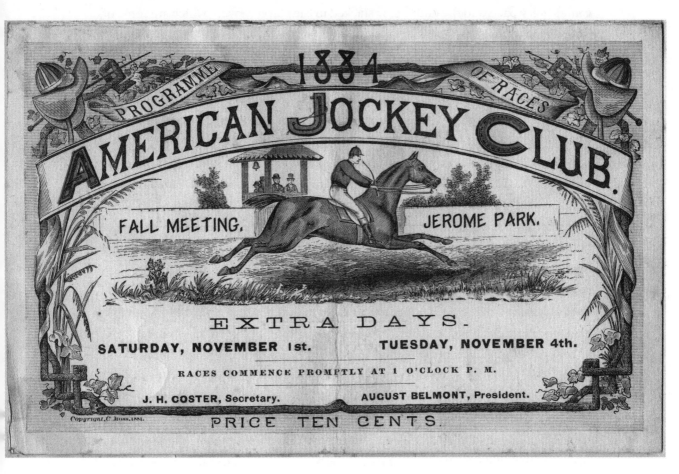

American Jockey Club, fall meeting, Jerome Park; racing form, November 4, 1884

helped save the Wild West from bankruptcy and inspired Cody to embark on one of his most successful business endeavors.

Originally invented in southwestern France, the game of faro was extremely popular almost from the onset. The game at that time was pronounced "pharaoh" or "pharaon." Initially banned in France in 1691, the game continued to be quite popular in England. Faro's popularity stemmed from the ease at which one learned to play, the game's quick pace, and the odds being stacked in the player's favor (which are some of the best for all gambling games).[13]

Faro spread to the United States in the mid-nineteenth century, becoming the most widespread and popular gambling card game in the country. Faro was played in almost every gambling hall in the Old West from 1825 to 1915. The game eventually was considered the most prevalent form of gambling, surpassing all other forms combined in terms of money wagered each year.[14]

A game of faro, often referred to as a "faro bank," was played with a single deck of playing cards. One person was designated the "banker" or dealer, and an indeterminate number of players, known as "punters," participated. Chips, called "checks," could be purchased by the punter from the banker. Bet values and limits were then set by the house. The faro table was typically oval, covered with green baize, and had a cutout for the banker. A board was placed on top of the table with one suit of cards, traditionally the suit of spades, adhered to it in numerical order. Each player laid his stake on one of the thirteen cards on the layout. Players could place multiple bets and could bet on multiple cards simultaneously by placing their bet between cards or on specific card edges.[15]

A deck of cards was then shuffled and placed inside a "dealing box," which was a mechanical device known as a "shoe" and used to prevent manipulations of the draw by the banker and intended to ensure players a fair game. The first card in the dealing box was usually called the "soda" and was discarded, leaving fifty-one cards in play. The dealer then drew two cards, the first of which was called the "banker's card" and was placed on the right side of the dealing box. The next card was called the "player's card" and placed on the left of the shoe.[16]

The banker's card was the "losing card," regardless of its suit, and all bets placed on the layout's card with the same denomination as the banker's card were lost by the players and won by the bank. The player's card was the "winning card." All bets placed on the layout card with the same denomination were returned to the players with an even money payout by the bank (a dollar bet won a dollar). If the card a player bet on was not drawn, the player's money would be returned to him and he was free to bet with it on the next hand.[17]

Faro was a fast-paced game, and its ease of play allowed for several players to participate at once. The simple rules and the nearly even odds in favor of the players only heightened the game's appeal. Often there would be so many players at a table there was nowhere for anyone to sit.

Faro, however, was notoriously crooked, and nearly everyone who played the game cheated at it. In a fair game the house's edge was low, so bankers increasingly resorted to cheating the players to improve the profitability of the game for the house. Crooked faro equipment was so popular that many companies began supplying gaffed dealing boxes specially designed so bankers could cheat players. The grift was so rampant that many gambling strategy books and guides at the time reported "[that] not a single honest faro bank could be found in the United States."[18]

Dealers often rigged decks with textured cards, allowing them to create paired cards in the deck while giving the illusion of thorough shuffling.[19] Rigged dealing boxes also came in several variants. Typically they allowed the dealer to see the next card prior to the deal, by use of a small mirror or prism visible only to the dealer. If the next card was heavily bet, the box could allow the dealer to draw two cards in one draw, thus hiding the card that would have paid.[20] The dealer could also, when he knew the next card to win, surreptitiously slide a player's bet off the winning card if it was on the dealer's side of the layout. At a hectic faro table, the banker could often get away with this.[21]

Players would routinely cheat as well. Their techniques employed distraction and sleight-of-hand, and usually involved moving their stake to a winning card, or at least off the losing card, without being detected.[22]

There is some question as to what exact date Evelyn Booth and Buffalo Bill Cody became first acquainted, but there is no doubt it was the game of faro that brought them into the same circle of influence. During the winter of 1884, Salsbury and Cody decided to keep the Wild West show in operation. It was not normal business practice to operate an outdoor spectacle like the Wild West during the winter months, but both Bill and Salsbury felt there was money to be made if they could find a quality spot to stay and perform where the weather would not be an issue.

So on December 6, 1884, after performing in Vicksburg, Mississippi, Bill's Wild West troupe boarded a boat and began winding their way down the Mississippi River to New Orleans. Buffalo Bill, meanwhile, separated from his Wild West performers and hustled by rail to the Crescent City in order to view the exposition grounds and make accommodations for his employees before they arrived.[23]

With his departure from the show troupe, Buffalo Bill needed to hire someone to take charge of securing transportation for the Wild West performers' trip to New Orleans. Leaning on old alliances, Cody turned to his longtime friend "Pony" Bob Haslam. This decision ended up being a total disaster for the Wild West. Throughout Cody's life, he was generous to a fault with friends, employees, and family. Cody never forgot his childhood friends or the people he worked with while following the road to international fame. The Little Sure Shot herself, Annie Oakley, once said of Cody's blind generosity, "He was totally unable to resist any claim for assistance that came to him or refuse any mortal in distress."[24] This was exactly the case for Cody's hiring of Haslam.

Pony Bob was a friend of Buffalo Bill's from their days working for the Pony Express. Bob was hired by the Pony Express as a teenager, helped build the stations, and was assigned the Nevada run from Friday's Station (State Line) to Buckland Station, seventy-five miles to the east. Haslam is credited with having made the longest round-trip journey of any Pony Express rider in the history of the company.

The story goes that at Buckland Station, Haslam's relief rider was so badly frightened over the supposed Indian threat he refused to take the mail. Stepping up, Haslam agreed to take the relief rider's mail all the way to Smith's Creek, amassing a total distance of 190 miles without rest. Then, after reaching Smith's Creek and resting for nine hours, Bob retraced his route with the westbound mail. At Cold Springs he found Indians had raided the place, killing the station keeper and running off all the stock. Evading the hostiles, Haslam reached Buckland Station, completing a 380-mile round-trip, the longest on record. This ride was an important contribution to the fastest trip ever made by the Pony Express. Legend also has it that one of the messages Pony Bob transported was a copy of Abraham Lincoln's 1861 inaugural address.[25]

Unfortunately for Buffalo Bill and his Wild West, Cody discovered Pony Bob was nowhere near as good at plotting a course down the Mississippi River as he was at riding mustangs. In desperate need of a job, Haslam begged Buffalo Bill for work. In an act of kindness toward his old buddy, Cody hired Haslam as the advance agent for the Wild West show. In the position of advance agent, Haslam selected the performance grounds for the enterprise and arranged transportation for the troupe. When charting a course down the Mississippi River, Pony Bob hired a riverboat and a navigator in Cincinnati, Ohio, to ferry the performers and equipment. Unfortunately for the whole Wild West enterprise, the navigator proved as incompetent in his position as Pony Bob.[26]

Upon arriving in New Orleans on December 8, 1884, Cody received a telegram containing news of complete disaster. On the preceding day, while steaming south toward the Crescent City, the boat carrying Bill's Wild West troupe, performing animals, and paraphernalia collided with another vessel, sinking the ship and almost drowning everyone on board. Apparently, after the collision the boat captain ran the ship ashore. He quickly proceeded to patch the damage to the boat and then set sail down the river once more.[27]

After traveling a short distance, the ship sank under thirty feet of water. When the vessel sank into the river, the famous Deadwood Stagecoach was nearly lost and world-champion trap shooter Captain Adam Henry Bogardus narrowly escaped with his life.[28] Recalling the calamity, Buffalo Bill, who estimated the monetary loss to be around $20,000, said, "We lost all our personal effects, including wagons, camp equipage, arms, ammunition, donkeys, buffaloes, and one elk."[29]

After learning of the accident, Buffalo Bill frantically telegraphed his show manager, Nate Salsbury. Nate, who was touring across the country with his Troubadours, was preparing to go onstage and sing at Denver's Tabor Opera House when he received Cody's terse telegram: OUTFIT AT THE BOTTOM OF THE RIVER. WHAT DO YOU ADVISE? Initially shaken by the news, Salsbury rushed to the speaking tube and shouted to the conductor in the orchestra pit, "Play that symphony again and a little harder, while I think for a minute." After a moment of contemplation, Salsbury told the messenger to telegraph Cody: GO TO NEW ORLEANS, REORGANIZE AND OPEN ON YOUR REGULAR DATE. [I] HAVE WIRED YOU FUNDS."[30] With the money sent to him by Salsbury, Buffalo Bill regained the majority of what he lost and opened his show in New Orleans on time.

Remarking on Haslam's job performance as advance agent, Salsbury said, "Pony Bob had as little judgment in such matters as any man I have ever met in my whole life. And while he was perfectly devoted to the service he undertook, he had not the slightest fitness for the work. He blundered along in a haphazard kind of way until he reached New Orleans, but he was sharp enough to send back the rosiest kind of reports on the condition of the country through which the route was laid."[31]

Among all this hardship for the Wild West, on March 13, 1885, Booth and his companions arrived in the Crescent City. Here was where Booth and Cody's paths would cross. While playing a game of faro, Booth was joined at the table by a man named Frank B. "Yank" Adams. It was through this man that Booth and his companions would gain an introduction to Buffalo Bill Cody. Adams was a professional carom billiards player who specialized in the sport of finger billiards. Finger billiards, or digital billiards, as it was commonly known, was a style of pool played in which a player directly manipulated the balls with his hands, instead of using an implement such as a cue stick. This was often done by twisting the ball between one's thumb and middle finger.[32]

Adams, who was sometimes billed as the "Digital Billiard Wonder," has been referred to by pool historians as the "greatest of all digit billiards players" and the "champion digital billiardist of the World."[33] Yank is also seen by many historians as the "greatest exhibition player who ever lived." Adams's exhibitions drew audiences of one thousand or more at a time, leaving standing room only, even in small venues.[34]

Largely self-taught, Adams amassed a large repertoire of finger billiards shots. He began to give performances in New York City. Later Adams traveled extensively, giving exhibitions and taking on challengers in cities across the United States and in Europe. During his travels, Adams performed before the Cornelius Vanderbilt family, the Jay Gould family, three US presidents, the Prince of Wales in London, and the Comte de Paris.[35]

After meeting Yank Adams for the first time, Evelyn Booth remarked about his billiard skills, writing, "Made the acquaintance of Pat Sheedy, who was very civil. Found out several new sporting houses [and] Pat introduced us to a friend of his, Yank Adams, proprietor of the Chicago Sporting Journal and a wonder at finger billiards."[36]

The connection between Buffalo Bill Cody and Yank Adams is one that is not entirely clear. However, both Yank and Bill were mutual friends with a man named Dr. Frank Powell, which is more than likely the source of their friendship. In the early days of Powell's medical practice, he was assigned to the post at Fort McPherson, Nebraska, next to the town of North Platte. Buffalo Bill was living in North Platte at the time, so their paths eventually crossed.[37]

Part of Powell's duties as fort surgeon was accompanying patrols in Indian country, a task that earned him the nickname "Surgeon Scout." It is possible Powell met Buffalo Bill on patrol or at a Masonic Lodge. After becoming friends with Cody, Powell eventually joined Buffalo Bill and Texas Jack Omohundro on a buffalo hunt. After this event Cody often remarked that he and Powell were "blood brothers."[38]

After leaving Nebraska, Powell subsequently practiced medicine in La Crosse, Wisconsin, in the early 1880s. While in La Crosse Powell served as mayor and ran unsuccessfully for governor on a populist ticket.[39] During his two years in office as mayor, Powell gathered a party of famous hunters to impress his constituency. Members of that hunting party included Buffalo Bill Cody and Yank Adams. The hunters were, of course, willing to show their skills with firearms to the gathering crowds. Powell, who was also a marksman, held his own with these famous sportsmen participating in displays of pistol-handling prowess. [40]

Whether they met through Doc Powell or through their work in the entertainment industry, Yank and Bill clearly knew each other. Evelyn Booth, when he gained a formal introduction to Buffalo Bill, wrote in his journal, "We four: Cody, Yank, Doc, and I went up to his camp to have some shooting and spent a very enjoyable day. Neither of us tried very hard in the shooting and a match was arranged for the following Saturday."[41]

After this initial shooting competition, the first of two official matches took place between Buffalo Bill and Evelyn Booth on March 28, 1885. "It was terribly windy which prevented accurate shooting," Booth said of the first match. "I won [by] three birds killing 40 to 37. Bill immediately challenged me again to shoot on the following Wednesday, the day appointed for his benefit, and another match was arranged."[42] A separate source states that Booth shot forty clay pigeons to Bill's thirty-nine in that first match.[43] The second contest took place on April 1, 1885, before three thousand spectators at New Orleans's exposition grounds. Buffalo Bill narrowly won the rematch, causing Booth to fume, "The return match was shot off with the following result, Bill 47 Self 46, though three were counted to him which he never touched."[44]

Although the outcome of the match was contentious, the two men became fast friends. They spent several evenings with the Wild West cowboys getting drunk, smashing glasses, and tussling with local police. The riotous living, however, could not disguise Cody's obvious financial troubles. The Wild West's woes prompted Booth to remark, "I fear the Honorable Cody is having a bad time of it as there are hardly any spectators and his expenses must be very heavy."[45] Cody himself said of the fiscal volatility, "The New Orleans exposition did not prove the success that many of its promoters anticipated and the expectations of Mr. Salsbury and myself were alike disappointed, for at the end of the winter we counted our losses at about $60,000."[46]

Needing a new business angle, Cody told Booth he wanted to take the Wild West overseas to London. Booth intimated his influence on Cody's decision, saying, "He is very anxious to take the whole show over to England next spring and I have had several talks with him about it and am going to make inquiry on the other side."[47]

At this point the seed of success in Europe was firmly planted in Cody's mind. Buffalo Bill noted in his memoir, "Though the idea of transplanting our exhibition, for a time, to England had frequently occurred to us, the importance of such an undertaking was enlarged by and brought us to a more favorable consideration of the project by repeated suggestions from prominent persons of America, and particularly by urgent invitations extended by distinguished Englishmen."[48]

Returning to America in 1886, Booth kept his promise to Buffalo Bill. On January 8 of that year, Booth, Cody, and Salsbury entered a lucrative partnership in which Booth paid a sum of $30,000 to Cody and Salsbury. In exchange, Booth became a one-third owner of "all livestock and other effects." Under further terms of the contract Booth would receive "25 percent of the profits from all sources connected with the enterprise." Cody and Salsbury shared the remaining 75 percent.[49]

Buffalo Bill remained in complete control of "all the Cow-boys, Mexicans, Indians, and Hostlers connected with the enterprise." Salsbury retained control of all "advertising, purchasing, the camp Department of said enterprise, and the regulation of the affairs of the Box Office." Each of the three men deposited $5,000 in the Merchant's Loan and Trust Company Bank of Chicago as a reserve fund. The agreement was to run three years.[50]

In June, the Wild West traveled north to New York's Staten Island. There Cody recouped most of his New Orleans losses, playing to large crowds at Erastina, the magnificent resort grounds of Erastus Wiman, former manager of a large mercantile company and president of the Great Northwestern Telegraph Co. of Canada.[51]

In 1887 those "prominent persons of America" that Cody mentioned in his memoir floated the idea of holding an American Exhibition, a world's fair held in West Brompton, London, in the same year of Queen Victoria's Golden Jubilee. The American Exhibition was an incredible success, and because of it Buffalo Bill became the most recognized American in the world, and the most requested guest of British royalty.[52]

Program from Buffalo Bill's Wild West in Europe, 1887

The Wild West show remained a major attraction in the United Kingdom until its final performance in 1906. After acquiring fame and great success abroad, Buffalo Bill apparently no longer needed financial assistance from Booth and allowed his contract, and their friendship, to lapse at the end of their three-year agreement.[53]

Though it would experience further financial wobbles, Buffalo Bill's Wild West would outlive Booth. Through the 1890s the wealthy Englishman continued to live the sporting man's life. He wagered on boxing title fights, sought travel adventures across America, and eventually owned ranchland in Wyoming. After a brief stint in Canada's Klondike with his wife, Lola, Booth ventured to Oregon, where in August 1901 he died from burns he received in a brush fire. He was only forty-one years old.[54]

Booth's contributions to Buffalo Bill's Wild West are worth remembering. This little-known English gent provided a source of income to the enterprise at a time of fiscal uncertainty, and Booth was one of the men who helped Cody hatch the idea of an overseas tour, which transformed the Wild West into an international phenomenon.

CHAPTER 8
Hail to the King!

Suggestions to travel with his Wild West overseas by individuals like Evelyn Booth eventually caused Cody to take a chance at success in a foreign land. The year 1887, when Bill and his troupe sailed to England, was a significant one because of the Golden Jubilee celebrating fifty years of Queen Victoria's reign. One of the more significant events taking place that year in honor of the queen was the American Exhibition, a showcase the Wild West eventually became a participant in. The Exhibition was like a world's fair, with a focus on displaying the latest in American agricultural, mechanical, and textile products as well as new inventions and innovations.[1]

Some of the advances on display were Singer sewing machines and Acme button-hole appliances. The Exhibition also sported a diorama of New York City and paintings from celebrated landscape artist Albert Bierstadt. The main attraction, however, eventually became Buffalo Bill's Wild West. Author Mark Twain said of the event, "The American Exhibition will be the first time that Europeans saw something truly American."[2]

In February 1887 Nate Salsbury received an inquiry from the Exhibition's organizers concerning the participation of Buffalo Bill's Wild West in the event. After a series of telegrams and messages between the two parties, the organizers made it official and invited the Wild West to be part of the Exhibition.[3] With the Wild West show making its way to London, Cody and Evelyn Booth's idea finally came to fruition.

Before leaving, Bill received a commission as a colonel and aide-de-camp in the Nebraska National Guard by Governor John M. Thayer.[4] Bill, ever the opportunist,

Buffalo Bill's Wild West on parade in New York City, circa 1884

would go on to use the title of "Colonel" for the rest of his days, which lent him a great deal of clout. Bill was also presented with a gold, jeweled sword by officers of the US Army, many of whom he served with during the Indian Wars.[5]

On March 31, Buffalo Bill and his entourage boarded a steamship named *State of Nebraska* and began the voyage to England. Shipping Buffalo Bill's Wild West from the docks of New York to the UK represented an enormous undertaking. The trip saw the transportation of 250 animals, one hundred cowboys and cowgirls, ninety-seven Indians including Black Elk and Chief Red Shirt, and numerous African American and Mexican entertainers.[6]

More than ten thousand people assembled in the streets near the New York pier to wish the Americans well on their trip across the Atlantic. Accompanying the *Nebraska* was a flotilla of over one hundred steamboats, yachts, and tugboats that chugged alongside the steamship until it reached the New York Bay. It was reported that many of the Indians in Cody's troupe were frightened by the journey.[7] In their defense, this would have been not only the first time for many of them to board a boat, but also the first time any of them had even seen an ocean.

The *State of Nebraska* disembarked at Albert Dock on April 15, 1887. While the Wild West troupe was braving the choppy seas of the Atlantic, their London hosts were busily constructing the exhibition hall and performing grounds for their arrival. The main gallery, after construction, measured about 1,280 feet in length and was in West Brompton, London, at Earl's Court. The entire American Exhibition encompassed nearly six acres of land, including the performance grounds where Buffalo Bill's Wild West would hold center stage.[8]

The exterior of the gallery was made of stone and embellished with large medallions embossed with the likenesses of presidents George Washington, Abraham Lincoln, and Grover Cleveland. These medallions were accentuated by other American symbols like eagles and flags. The exhibition grounds encompassed eight vast halls that were deemed "fireproof." These halls displayed several artworks and sculpture created by numerous American artists. The main exhibition hall contained manufactured goods, machinery, firearms, instruments, and books. There was even an "American Bar" featuring mixologists from New York who prepared American-style cocktails for attendees.[9]

Buffalo Bill set up camp near the performance grounds, where he and his troupe became the object of much discussion and ogling. They were visited by many high

Vaquero shooting over horse, circa 1900

society types and onlookers who wanted to catch their first glimpse of a real American cowboy and a real American Indian. And, as described by many of London's newspapers, Bill's accommodations for his troupe and for himself were none too shabby. The tents were outfitted with furniture and beds along with a cooking stove. The Indian's had tepees they adorned with colors and drawings of bison and other sacred animals. Most of the Londoners found everyone courteous and outgoing, which endeared Buffalo Bill and his company to the English people immediately.[10]

Many of the Indians toured the city of London and interacted with the populous while visiting many of the sights as construction of the exhibition grounds took place. It was reported that they were particularly impressed with the Tower of London Palace and Westminster Abby. The Sioux chief Red Shirt told local reporters that he and his entourage enjoyed the Tower so much that they wanted to make a return trip when they had time to do so.[11]

During the days leading up to the opening, Buffalo Bill took time to entertain guests and roving reporters who showed up to the construction site to report on the building's progress and to mingle with the cowboys and Indians. He never missed a beat, doing exclusive interviews for select newspapers and constantly hyping the upcoming show with his interviews. Bill was at his most quotable and an absolute promotional machine.[12]

The American Exhibition officially opened on May 9, 1887, and Cody's Wild West soon became the centerpiece of the exhibition. Originally, it was to be part of the state of Colorado's contribution but found success separating itself.[13] In some ways, Buffalo Bill's Wild West was the saving grace of the Exhibition. Many of the British critics of the show noted the American art on display had "yet to justify its existence."[14] And though the American machinery and inventions on display fared a little better in the reviews, they were still seen as lackluster exhibits.

Because of the success of the Wild West, Buffalo Bill was invited to tea with the celebrated author and poet Oscar Wilde. He also had a drinking session with the renowned actor Henry Irving. Eventually, Bill enjoyed an extravagant dinner with the illustrious Churchill family (the same lineage that gave the world political leader Winston Churchill).[15]

Cody and Chief Red Shirt also toured parliament, where they were greeted with great admiration. Buffalo Bill felt the Wild West's time in England influenced many Europeans to set about reading and educating themselves on the history of the

American West. Cody even hosted dinners for European dignitaries featuring American cuisine replete with cornbread cakes and Boston pork and beans.[16]

Noting the excitement and comradery brought by Buffalo Bill's Wild West, the *London Times* stated, "Buffalo Bill has done his part in bringing America and England together."[17] The Wild West remained in England for the entirety of 1887. They traveled from London to Birmingham and eventually to Manchester.[18] Over the Fourth of July, the members of the Wild West celebrated with European dignitaries at a special dinner where the two sides "buried the hatchet," so to speak, and enjoyed one another's fellowship on that most American of holidays.[19]

During the American Exhibition's run throughout 1887, Buffalo Bill's Wild West held command performances for the Prince and Princess of Wales. In fact, the Prince of Wales, later King Edward VII, requested a private preview of the Wild West performance on May 5, 1887. After seeing the Wild West show, he arranged a command performance on May 11 for Queen Victoria.[20]

Legend has it that at the end of the performance for the Queen, Buffalo Bill rode his faithful horse Charley up to the foot of the viewing box where Victoria was seated, took his hat off as a sign of respect, and presented her with a lowered American flag. Victoria, in response to the gesture, got to her feet and saluted Bill and Old Glory. Whether this happened is still a matter of debate. The Queen, however, did record her high acclaim for the Wild West show within the pages of her personal journal. Interestingly, the smashing success of Buffalo Bill's Wild West overseas was also seen by many critics as a great stroke of diplomacy.[21]

Buffalo Bill and his entourage eventually returned home to the United States on May 5, 1888. Upon their arrival the troupe received a hero's welcome. All told, the London tour accounted for more than three hundred performances and over 2.5 million tickets sold.[22]

Sadly for Buffalo Bill, his faithful horse Charley, who performed so well for Queen Victoria and whom Bill had ridden for fifteen years, died on the return trip to America. The horse performed so admirably during the American Exhibition that several London papers did multiple write-ups on the steed. Charley, Bill reported with intense sadness, was buried at sea in the middle of the Atlantic.[23]

In 1888 Buffalo Bill's Wild West completed the show season by touring throughout several states, ending in Richmond, Virginia. The shows were packed with adoring fans and onlookers. While several of the Indians stayed with the show, others returned

Wild West group on a barge in Germany, circa 1890

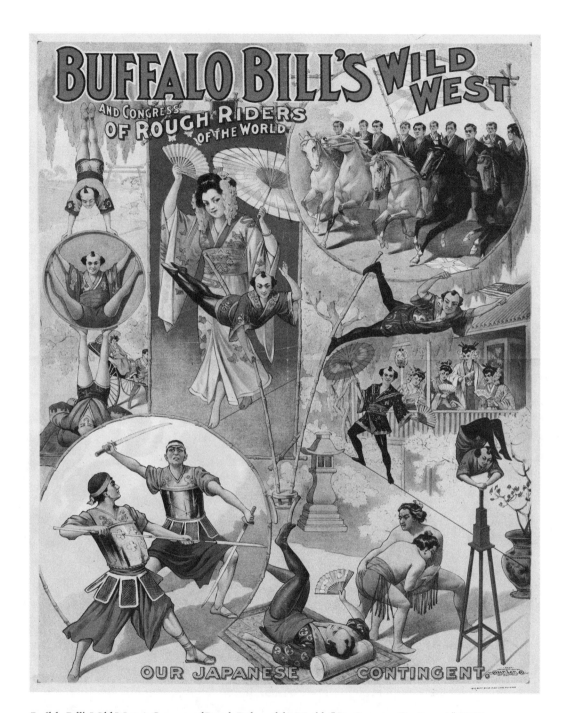

Buffalo Bill's Wild West & Congress of Rough Riders of the World: "Our Japanese Contingent," 1907

to their reservations. When the Wild West troupe completed their 1888 tour, they received a special reception with President Grover Cleveland in the White House. While there, Cody was celebrated as an international sensation. After the celebration the troupe went their separate ways. Buffalo Bill returned to his home in North Platte, and Salsbury went on the road with his Troubadours.[24]

Following the winter of 1888–1889, Buffalo Bill and Salsbury decided to take the Wild West back to Europe. On this occasion, however, they decided a tour of the entire continent was the only way to outdo their previous endeavor. The two seasoned businessmen planned to open the entertainment season in France for Paris's Exposition Universelle. This exhibition was a six-month centennial celebration and remembrance of the French Revolution. It was also where the Eiffel Tower premiered.[25]

In May 1889 Buffalo Bill's Wild West embarked on what would be a five-month stay in France. At this time, Arizona John Burke and Nate Salsbury felt a tour of the rest of mainland Europe was important to capitalize on the momentum of the previous season.[26]

Burke and Salsbury convinced Buffalo Bill to take his troupe through southern France, Barcelona, Sardinia, Corsica, Naples, Rome, Florence, and other Italian cities. They also held performances in Austria and Germany through 1889 and into 1890. The Wild West toured through Holland, Belgium, England, Wales, and Scotland and eventually returned to England for a command performance during the summer of 1892.[27]

Bill's schedule became so packed on the European tour that at one point he visited the Tomb of General Marie-Joseph Paul Yves Roch Gilbert du Motier de Lafayette, hosted a meal for dignitaries at the Wild West camp, participated in an afternoon performance, attended a Legation reception, returned for an evening performance, and attended a reception for US Minister Whitelaw Reid all in a single day.[28]

Buffalo Bill's Wild West spent five years in Europe putting on arena shows during the summer and indoor pageants through the winter months. At this time, Cody went to great lengths to present his Wild West as a historic retelling of the settling of the American West. He also sought to give European audiences the opportunity to experience not only the lives and culture of cowboys and pioneers but of American Indians as well.[29]

In his sets Cody focused on re-creating the cities of the Great Plains, like Omaha and Denver, which were completely different from their European counterparts and their eastern American equivalents. Europeans found these cities, stories, and people fascinating.[30]

For Europeans, it was commonplace to see castles with massive spires and soldiers clad in suits of armor seemingly on every street corner in every hamlet or city. But sharpshooting cowboys decked out head to toe in buckskins and Indians in full war-bonnets with painted faces participating in ceremonial dances were not only intriguing but absolutely enthralling to them.

As word of the unique performances spread, Europeans flocked by the thousands to buy tickets for the chance to attend Buffalo Bill's Wild West. Upon their return trip from Europe in 1893, American audiences began to take notice and snatched up tickets to experience this once-in-a-lifetime event. That same year Cody changed the name of his outfit from Buffalo Bill's Wild West to Buffalo Bill's Wild West and Rough Riders of the World. Along with this name change, he incorporated several types of horsemen into the show's repertoire. Buffalo Bill was now employing not only the traditional American cowboys and Indians, but Turks, gauchos, Arabs, Mongols, and Georgians who displayed their varied skills and uniquely colorful costumes.[31]

Another key factor to Buffalo Bill becoming the king of all entertainers was the World's Columbian Exposition, held in 1893 in the city of Chicago. Featured prominently in Erik Larson's *New York Times* best-selling popular history, *The Devil in the White City*, the Columbian Exposition was a singularly historic event.

Bidding to be the host city began in 1882. The contract was eventually awarded in 1890 to the Windy City. Construction of the event grounds included facades made of a mixture of plaster, cement, and a fibrous substance referred to as "staff." When the buildings reached completion, they were all painted white. Streetlights had also come into use at this time, and they were used liberally throughout the establishment to illuminate the exposition grounds at night.[32]

Accompanied by the brightness of the streetlamps and the buildings slathered with gallons of fresh pallid paint, the exposition structures glowed quite brightly. This assortment of buildings stood out even more when compared with the tenement homes surrounding them. Because of this fact, the entire structure was summarily dubbed by the Chicago press as "The White City."[33]

The fair, however, was not only historic for its White City architecture but also for the multitude of innovations, inventions, and introduction of current staples to Americans' everyday lives. Some of the firsts at the fair were the introduction of Cream of

La Rana nel Wild West (*alternate title:* The Frog in the Wild West), *created by M. Cetto, 1906*

Wild West Show cowgirls, 1901

Wheat, Juicy Fruit gum, Aunt Jemima pancake mix, Quaker Oats, Pabst Blue Ribbon beer, Vienna Sausages, brownies, and Hershey's milk chocolate.

Along with those potables, Frederick Jackson Turner debuted his "Frontier Thesis," in which Turner theorized that because of the advent of advanced American westward expansion the frontier had officially closed. George Washington Gale Ferris Jr. introduced his ferris wheel. An automatic dishwasher and the first version of the zipper debuted as well.[34]

The exposition, unfortunately, also became infamous for a serial killer who stalked its brilliantly lit streets. Herman Webster Mudgett, a confessed criminal, who traveled under the alias Dr. Henry Howard Holmes, was more commonly known as H. H. Holmes. Mudgett was proven responsible for nine confirmed murders and while incarcerated confessed to twenty-seven more.[35] It was reported he employed a mixed-use building that he owned and redesigned with hidden rooms and winding corridors to entrap his victims.[36]

Holmes's building was also designed with floor chutes connecting to the basement where he stored acid vats, quicklime, and a crematorium. In the cover of night, the villainous Holmes alleviated his victims of their flesh and internals, and in some cases the skeletons were then sold to medical schools.[37] It is believed he wandered the streets of the White City in order to entice and claim more victims. He was eventually captured and hanged for his heinous crimes in 1896.[38]

Amid all this fanfare and fright, however, one of America's greatest exhibitors was not included in the Columbian Exposition. Though he petitioned for quite some time for inclusion when he learned the exposition would be held in Chicago, Buffalo Bill Cody and his Wild West were excluded from the event. Perhaps it was because of a brash smugness purveyed by the fair's promoters that kept Bill and his troupe from participating. These men may have felt that a show whose premise was the celebration of the settling of the western American frontier was beneath them. They most likely saw the Wild West as entertainment for nothing more than hicks and rubes. But in any account, Buffalo Bill defied them all and threw the promoters' refusal back in their faces.

In the ultimate display of true Western defiance, Bill and his troupe saddled up their ponys and made their way to Chicago. Upon arrival, Bill set up his performance grounds just outside the edge of the exposition. Many of the promoters who refused the Wild West access to the Columbian Exposition were angry after discovering what

Cody had done. In response, Bill began skillfully syphoning spectators away from the exposition.[39]

Cody offered free admission to six thousand children of poor and underprivileged families, which he dubbed "the Playday of Waifs." He plastered the city with advertisements that led many who attended the Columbian Exposition to feel the experience was only complete if they also attended Buffalo Bill's Wild West. It was not a coincidence that the location Cody chose allowed for people interested in attending the White City to easily access Buffalo Bill's Wild West as well.[40]

Bill's promotion was so expertly executed, some attendees actually thought the Wild West was part of the Columbian Exposition experience, and when buying a ticket to one they were surprised to find it did not grant them entry to the other.[41] Bill outdid the exposition's promoters on one other note as well. He scheduled the Wild West to open on April 26, which happened to be six days before the world's fair was to open on May 1. He also scheduled his exhibition to run one day longer, closing on October 31.[42]

The Wild West's time in Chicago caused Cody's popularity to surge in the United States.[43] After establishing himself as a sensation overseas, Bill now became a household name across North America. Never one to not capitalize on the moment, Bill returned to Europe for another successful run, and would eventually tour the continent four more times between 1902 and 1906.[44]

Life on the road, however, had its drawbacks, especially when it came to Cody's home life. The many hours Bill spent away from his family caused his marriage to suffer. There has been much speculation as to Bill's infidelity, especially involving the stage actresses he employed. Because of that, his marriage to Louisa Federici was damaged by numerous separations and eventually by Cody attempting to divorce her in 1905.[45]

During their divorce proceedings, Bill told a story in which he claimed Louisa poisoned him on Christmas Eve 1900. He said the poison caused him to collapse to the ground and stifled his cries for help by rendering him unable to speak. Bill eventually recovered from this episode, but he asserted his wife had been slowly poisoning him over a period of months.[46]

Cody stated in the court transcripts that the poison Louisa bought was a concoction known as Dragon's Blood. This was supposedly "a Victorian-era anti-abuse-type medication designed to open the "sluices" at both ends." Bill claimed she procured the

Left to right: unidentified man, William F. Cody, Arta Cody, Louisa Cody, Orra Maude Cody, Colonel Torrance, Mr. and Mrs. Sayette G. Hicks, 1878

potion from a Gypsy traveler who told her that "by feeding it to him it would make him love her again." Responding to the accusation, Louisa said that she had never heard of a concoction called Dragon's Blood and denied giving Bill the tonic.[47]

Bill did not stop there, however. He went on to accuse Louisa of having poisoned his prize stag hounds, which he received from the czar of Russia. She refuted this by telling the judge the hounds were poisoned by mistake when food doused with strychnine was put out to kill rats and mistakenly eaten by the dogs.[48]

After hearing all the evidence, the presiding judge dismissed Cody's claim, stating he believed Bill simply overindulged in alcohol on Christmas Eve 1900. The judge also stated he believed Louisa had given him nothing more than a serum to help cure his hangover. He eventually sided with Louisa and decided not to annul the marriage. It was also common knowledge that Louisa hated her husband's love of wine and spirits and believed he was having affairs with some of the Wild West's female performers. This more than likely led to the judge's decision.[49]

Some historians have noted of Louisa's jealousy that "she was jealous of all his fine friends, of the carousals at his ranch in Wyoming, of the adulation from adoring crowds he received, and of the long journeys overseas on which he never took her." On one particular occasion in 1887, it was reported Bill kissed each of the showgirls goodbye at the end of the Wild West's touring season, making Louisa so furious she never forgot it.[50] Not too long after the divorce court ruling, Bill began suffering from extremely debilitating headaches. To combat them, he began taking special "powders" that he imported from Canada. Today it is believed that these "powders" contributed to his kidney failure.[51]

Buffalo Bill certainly loved the ladies, but many of the problems he and Louisa experienced in their marriage can be attributed to the deaths of the couple's children. Their son Kit Carson Cody was only six years old when he died from scarlet fever at the Codys' home in Rochester, New York. Bill caught a train home from a performance with his Combination after Louisa sent him word of the boy's illness. He arrived just in time to have the young boy die in his arms. The grief they experienced was devastating for the couple and the reason Bill took Johnny Baker under his wing as a foster son.[52]

The sorrow the two endured did not end with the death of Kit, however. The Codys' third child, Orra Maude Cody, died at the tender age of eleven. They buried their young daughter alongside their son in Mount Hope Cemetery in Rochester.[53]

James A. Bailey

They received yet another brutal blow before their divorce proceedings in 1904 when their oldest child, Arta Lucille Cody, died at the age of thirty-eight from appendicitis. Arta would also be buried near her brother and sister in Mount Hope Cemetery.[54]

The sudden death of Arta was a deep wound and difficult for both Codys to recover from, and each turned their grief into anger. While traveling by train to the funeral, Louisa accused Bill of "breaking Arta's heart and causing her death."[55] Bill tried to appease his wife and told her otherwise, but she continued to harp at him. On the return train trip from the funeral, Louisa made a spectacle of herself at the Auditorium Hotel, berating Buffalo Bill and his sisters in front of a crowd of onlookers. In 1905, unable to deal with Louisa's anguish, Buffalo Bill filed the divorce proceedings that were never recognized. The Codys' last remaining child, Irma, lived until 1918, dying at the age of thirty-five, one year after the death of her father. Sadly, for Louisa, she outlived her husband and all her children, events that were no doubt difficult to endure.[56]

Along with the turmoil in his personal life, Buffalo Bill also made a series of financial missteps around the turn of the century that crippled his businesses. Following the Wild West's thrilling success during the Columbian Exposition in 1893 and the many successful tours of Europe, Nate Salsbury began to suffer from declining health. Because of this, he struck a deal with James A. Bailey, who, along with P. T. Barnum, was one of the original creators of the Barnum and Bailey Circus. Bailey had taken control of the circus following Barnum's death in 1891. Through this deal, Bailey became a subcontractor for the Wild West and took care of Salsbury's obligations for the show, which included scheduling performances and managing the affairs of the box office.[57]

It is interesting to note that at this time Cody and Salsbury were involved in another entertainment enterprise called Black America. This act was like the Wild West show but featured Black performers in all the roles. Unfortunately for Cody and Salsbury, the business venture was completely unsuccessful, losing nearly $78,000. This caused a rift between the men wherein each blamed the other for the show's failure.[58]

Much like the Black America venture, the agreement with Bailey also hurt Buffalo Bill's Wild West. Under Bailey's influence the Wild West stopped being advertised as an educational enterprise and started being surrounded by grifters, hustlers, and circus sideshows. Bailey also worked to keep the Wild West out of competition with his other circus businesses. In doing so, his scheduling of events often put the Wild West at a disadvantage.[59]

Arab acrobats in the Wild West show, circa 1901

While Bailey was scheduling events for the Wild West, he also offered Buffalo Bill a lucrative contract to sever his business dealings with Salsbury. This caused an even greater fracture in their relationship. Bailey told Cody he would give him $50,000 upfront and $1,000 a week to break his agreements. Tempted by the offer, Cody eventually wrote a letter to Salsbury expressing his wish to break their contract and stated, "I have done the work & made the money. [I am ready] to go on my own."[60]

After receiving the letter, Salsbury quickly reminded Cody that Buffalo Bill's Wild West Company was a corporation he was part owner of, and Bill could not just abscond with the trademarked Buffalo Bill title. Salsbury also reminded Bill that he knew Cody had taken money from the company's coffers to support his failing real estate development projects in Wyoming, and those needed to be repaid too. Many letters with similar content were hurled back and forth between the two parties for a long period of time.[61]

Through these contentious conversations, however, Cody and Salsbury were eventually able to compromise and remained partners for another three years. During that period, Bill and Nate made plans to break from James Bailey and refocus on reinvigorating Buffalo Bill's Wild West. They wanted to take the enterprise away from the carnival atmosphere it had become and return the business back to the historical show it had once been. In fact, Salsbury wrote Cody, saying, "In three weeks and a little more we will be done with Bailey. . . ." Unfortunately for the two men, Salsbury died in 1902 before they could follow through with their plans.[62]

With the death of his longtime manager, Bill felt overwhelmed by the numerous responsibilities of the Wild West. So he continued to rely on James Bailey, who continued his same unethical practices. Bill also owed a good deal of money to Bailey for his services and continued to suffer from losses on his Wyoming property, mines in Arizona, and mismanagement of his personal finances. Because of the debts he shouldered, Cody decided to enter yet another partnership in 1909 with Gordon W. Lillie, better known under the stage name of Pawnee Bill.[63]

Lillie was a former Indian agent and was once an interpreter for the Pawnee Indians employed in Buffalo Bill's Wild West. He eventually left Cody's enterprise and formed an entertainment exhibition of his own titled "Pawnee Bill's Historical Wild West." Pawnee Bill found moderate success featuring unique exhibitions like Hindu escape artists and African and South American performers.[64]

When Cody and Lillie joined forces, their enterprise became known as "Buffalo Bill's Wild West Combined with Pawnee Bill's Far East." The entertainment spectacle was nicknamed in the press as the "Two Bills Show." Under this new partnership, Lillie bought out the remaining Bailey family's shares in the Wild West and reestablished Buffalo Bill as the figurehead of the show while he ran the day-to-day operations.[65]

This combined enterprise featured camels, elephants, and dancing girls, and brought in over $400,000 in profits. The new injection of cash allowed Cody to begin paying down what he owed to Lillie and reclaim his reputation as one of the world's greatest showmen.[66] Unfortunately for Buffalo Bill, he could not leave well enough alone and made one last financial misstep.

In 1913 Harry Tammen, owner of the *Denver Post* newspaper as well as the Sells-Floto Circus, met with Buffalo Bill while he was in Denver visiting his sister May Cody Decker, who was living in the Mile-High City at the time. Tammen offered Cody a loan of $20,000 to pay off an outstanding debt he owed to his partner, Gordon Lillie. As he had done with Salsbury, Bill did not recall that the "Two Bills Show" was a corporation and not solely owned by him. At the close of an unsuccessful 1913 season, Tammen demanded Bill repay the loan. When Cody was unable to come up with the cash, the Two Bills Show went bankrupt and all the remaining assets were subsequently sold to Tammen. Taking control of the enterprise, the newspaper tycoon officially dispersed Buffalo Bill's Wild West and forced Cody to perform in his circus shows during the 1914 season.[67]

The Sells-Floto enterprise was a miserably poor excuse for a circus, and Cody spent most of his time trying to come up with a new idea to relaunch his Wild West, but nothing came to fruition. After spending the 1915 season with Sells-Floto in hopes of making enough money to relaunch his show, Cody decided he had had his fill of the third-rate circus and swore, "I'll never go out with this show again." After Cody stepped away, Tammen informed Cody he could not use the Buffalo Bill moniker unless he paid the newspaperman $5,000.[68]

To pay off the debt to Tammen and reclaim his name, Bill worked on a lecture circuit, speaking about the films he produced, and wrote a new autobiography that was eventually serialized in *Hearst's International* magazine. After pulling Tammen's boot off his throat, Bill joined the Miller and Arlington's Wild West Show Company, one of the last Wild West shows of any kind left.[69]

At this point in his life, Bill was pushing seventy and could hardly ride a horse. For most of his performances he rode around the arena in a carriage to salute the onlookers. Some reports say that after riding around the arena on a horse and waving his hat to introduce the circus, Bill would quickly ride offstage and be helped from his horse by Johnny Baker, who basically caught Cody as he fell from the saddle. By all accounts, Buffalo Bill enjoyed his time with this show because it incorporated many of the same themes of his original Wild West show. After the conclusion of the performing season, during the winter of 1916, Cody, who was quite ill at the time, visited his sister May Cody Decker in Denver. Sadly, Bill would die only a few months later, in January 1917, at the age of seventy.[70] His passing signaled not only the end of a great entertainment career but the loss of a true American icon.

Numerous historians contend that at the turn of the century Colonel William Frederick "Buffalo Bill" Cody was the single most famous person on earth. Certainly, he was the most recognized American in the world, even more so than several sitting presidents. Throughout his eight European tours, the Wild West played to packed houses all over the United Kingdom, Belgium, the Netherlands, Spain, Italy, in the ancient Roman amphitheater in Verona, and at the opening of the Eiffel Tower, to name just a few of the venues.[71]

Buffalo Bill left a lasting impression on Europe and its people. He gave the world something truly American in its origin, appearance, and portrayal. He brought the fading frontier and its people to an audience that was ready to accept and enjoy the stories born on the Great Plains of the American West.

As Bill brought recognition to his country, he won great admiration from his fellow Americans. In Cody, many found a hero and a man to admire. He was someone who had braved the western frontier, fought courageously in battle, and found great financial success making millions of people happy with his Wild West show. He was almost the embodiment of the American Dream.

In Cody's day these men and women lived in a world that was changing rapidly, and Buffalo Bill's Wild West was reminiscent of a time when the country was young and unsettled, a country that was full of life, wonder, and possibility with adventure waiting to be had. Buffalo Bill Cody was one of the most well-known citizens in the world, but above all he was an American. He was someone the country could hang its hat on and be proud to have representing them on such an enormous stage.

A good deal of Cody's success came from a combination of personal charisma and fortunate circumstances. He was in the right place at the right time when he was discovered by Ned Buntline. He was also blessed with the looks and personality that endeared him to fawning crowds. It is true he endured financial stumbles along with great success, but he was able to build an enterprise with a lasting effect on multiple generations during his seventy years of life and the decades following his death.

Bill Cody was not a man without faults, both in his professional and personal life. He did, however, try to treat people fairly and pay honest wages for honest work. He helped a woman, Annie Oakley, become his biggest star, treated American Indians as equals, and worked tirelessly to create an experience that would bring joy to people of all ages. Cody saw his show as a historical retelling of a shared American experience—perseverance, and the indomitable human spirit to overcome hardship and adversity. Audiences of all types identified with this message and fell in love with Buffalo Bill.

Parts of Buffalo Bill's show were certainly embellished and, in several instances, completely fabricated. However, there were kernels of truth in many of his reenactments, and most of the performers in his show were the genuine article. The Wild West show brought joy to the millions who witnessed it and allowed children to dream of something bigger than themselves. And for that, Cody should be commended.

CHAPTER 9
"Heroes Get Remembered but Legends Never Die"

Buffalo Bill led an incredible life that many of us can only dream of. He rode the open range when the West was truly wild. He garnered the highest praise through his military service, and eventually found great wealth and fame onstage and in arenas. Cody's life was full of great fortune, and great misfortune—the proverbial highs and lows. His was truly a life well lived. But all of this begs the question, what is Buffalo Bill's place in history? Or, more specifically, does he even have a place in history?

The 1993 film *The Sandlot*, produced by Twentieth Century Fox, revolves around a group of young boys who gather in a shabby neighborhood field to play baseball. The story takes place in the summer of 1962, and after a series of comedic events the boys unwittingly play a game with a ball stolen from the protagonist's father, which just so happens to be signed by baseball legend Babe Ruth.

While playing with the priceless ball, the boys hit it over a neighboring fence into the yard of a curmudgeon who owns a massive Great Dane referred to as "The Beast." This dog gobbles up all baseballs hit into his yard, including the Babe Ruth ball. After realizing their mistake, the boys make several attempts to retrieve the ball but are continually foiled by The Beast. Eventually one of the boys, named Benny Rodriguez, portrayed by actor Mike Vitar, has a prophetic dream in which he is visited by the ghost of Babe Ruth, portrayed by character actor Art LaFleur.

During the dream, Babe helps Benny realize he is destined to do something great, which in this case is jumping the fence and stealing the baseball from The Beast. Over the course of their dialogue, Babe tells Rodriguez, "Remember kid, there's heroes and

Reenactment of a stagecoach holdup in Cody, Wyoming. Photograph by F. J. Hiscock, July 4, 1908.

there's legends. Heroes get remembered but legends never die. . . ." For a silly coming-of-age comedy, this is a poignant and emotional moment. As applicable to a legendary athlete like Babe Ruth, so too do these words apply to a man like Buffalo Bill Cody.

Not only is Buffalo Bill Cody America's first superhero and celebrity spokesman, he was also one of the world's earliest film producers. His ideas and performances inspired countless children and adults to dream of the Wild West that once was. Buffalo Bill's Wild West show inspired Hollywood in its early days, and Bill even participated in several of the earliest film shorts. He formed the Buffalo Bill/Pawnee Bill Film Company and produced the moderately successful movie *The Life of Buffalo Bill*, released by Barnsdales Moving Pictures.[1]

Cody's voluminous biographies were also the basis for numerous movies, and his Wild West show influenced every type of motion picture, from Westerns and adventure flicks to romances and dramas. His mark on popular culture does not end with movies, however. Comic books evolved from the early dime novels where Buffalo Bill reigned as king. These fantastical stories featuring Buffalo Bill became the most basic building block for the comic book heroes who followed in his enormous footsteps.

The National Football League's Buffalo Bills, who are named after Cody, currently have an estimated worth of $1.6 billion and remain an extremely popular franchise.[2] The Buffalo team was originally part of the All-America Football Conference (AAFC) and in 1946 were nicknamed the "Bisons." To drum up fan interest, team owner James Breuil, of the Frontier Oil Company, in 1947 held a contest to rename the team. The winning entry suggested the "Bills" as the nickname.[3] Carrying the "frontier" theme even further, the winning contestant also offered that the team was "opening a new frontier in sports in western New York." When the Buffalo Bills joined the new American Football League in 1960, the name of the city's earlier pro football entry was adopted.[4]

Another interesting tradition celebrating Buffalo Bill's legacy remaining today takes place in one of Denver's oldest restaurants. Founded in 1893, the Buckhorn Exchange, Denver's oldest continuously operating restaurant, celebrates the legacy of Cody with its annual Buffalo Bill look-alike contest. Among the displays of antique weapons, hundreds of mounted animal heads, and other assorted taxidermy on its bright red walls are dozens of photographs of men who have won the honor of being proclaimed the best Buffalo Bill impersonator. The Buckhorn Exchange also claims to have been visited by Buffalo Bill himself and to be the oldest operating liquor license in all of Denver.[5]

With numerous museums and institutions of research dedicated to his life and work, Bill remains a recognized and historically influential figure. Among the many accomplishments and monuments, however, there is one searing imprint left by his legacy. William Cody's historical significance lies solely with Buffalo Bill's Wild West. This entertainment enterprise shaped our vision of what the Old West once was. From settlers circling their wagons in defense against Indians to attacks by bandits on a stagecoach, William Cody is almost solely responsible for bringing us these Western tropes. Whether through movies, multiple forms of literature, or a shared collective consciousness, these images are ingrained in our minds. His impact on popular culture is universal, even for those who have never even heard of the man.

Without Buffalo Bill it is quite possible there would be no Hollywood, no superheroes, and no national idea of the Wild West. It has been said, "Buffalo Bill's Wild West portrayed Americans exactly as they wanted to see themselves—as heroes who only fought when provoked and who were merciful to their enemies."[6] In some ways, there is truth in this statement. But in many other ways, Cody gave his audiences several doses of historical truth mixed in with theatrical embellishments.

When reviewing Buffalo Bill's life, it is difficult at times to separate fact from fiction. As much as he tried to disassociate himself from the nickel weekly stories and their embellished myths, he never went out of his way to disprove them or point out that his real life had little if anything to do with the stories that flowed from Prentiss Ingraham's pen. However, it is this combined mix of truth and myth that has branded our national consciousness. Like any man, Cody's life was complicated. He had his faults and his strengths. His ups and his downs. These facts have been brought forth in this volume not to exhibit Bill's imperfections, however, but to illustrate his humanity. Despite his faults, Bill gave the world something lasting and well remembered.

As the years following the death of the old scout have accumulated into more than a century, the public's love affair with the Western genre has waxed and waned. In the earliest days of silent films, Westerns made for popular melodramas. Buffalo Bill himself was featured in films dating as far back as 1894. He was a writer on short subjects as well as an actor and producer in others. Perhaps if he had lived longer, Bill would have found success in the medium. In fact, he was involved in films in some capacity almost up to his death in 1917.

Paul Newman as Cody in Buffalo Bill and the Indians. *Archive photo dated July 11, 1976.*

Cody understood movies just as well as their creator, Thomas Edison. He realized the potential influence and power they had as an entertainment and information vessel. Following his death, Westerns became a staple of the silent film era. Most notably, the twelve-minute short the *Great Train Robbery*, released in 1903, is considered a milestone in filmmaking with its composite editing, on-location shooting, and frequent camera movements.[7]

Following a short period of decline, the genre sprang back into prominence in the late 1940s and 1950s. Actor John Wayne and director John Ford worked in tandem to make their marks on cinema with their numerous popular and profitable movie Westerns. The invention of television at this time also introduced the Western to the small screen.

The advent of the television Western drove the genre to new heights, introducing millions of Americans to tales of cowboys and Indians, which Buffalo Bill had earlier mythologized in his Wild West. In 1959 alone, at the genre's peak, there were twenty-six Westerns featured on television. As the 1950s gave way to the 1960s, the Western began to change with the times. The combination of the civil rights movement, the Vietnam War, and political protest irrevocably challenged a large part of the Western genre's appeal, which was based on its belief in set values.[8]

However, as it has always done, the Western adapted. During the 1960s, Sergio Leone's retelling of Akira Kurosawa's samurai tales as "spaghetti Westerns," starring the rugged Clint Eastwood, became prominent and popular. The "Man with No Name" trilogy included *A Fistful of Dollars, A Few Dollars More*, and *The Good, the Bad and the Ugly. The Magnificent Seven*, a remake of another Kurosawa tale, found a wide audience, and John Wayne, the king of the genre, eventually won an Academy award for his portrayal of the ultimate anti-hero, Rooster Cogburn, in *True Grit*.

Director Sam Peckinpah added to the darker and grittier side of the genre with many of his films, most notably 1969's *The Wild Bunch*. This movie in particular is seen as a hallmark for the modern Western. Violence and grimier characters were prominently featured by Peckinpah, which is viewed as a social commentary on the changing sensibilities of the decade. Those who have followed in Peckinpah's footsteps when creating Westerns today often mimic *The Wild Bunch* in style and character development.

The 1970s were a rough decade for the Western, but Buffalo Bill made a splash on the big screen in 1976's *Buffalo Bill and the Indians, or Sitting Bull's History Lesson*,

Members of the band for Buffalo Bill's Wild West Show pose with their instruments while touring with the show in Europe, circa 1892.

directed by Robert Altman and starred Paul Newman as the old scout. The 1980s also saw a slowdown in the production of Westerns aside from the occasional television movie or stand-alone film like John Fusco's *Young Guns* in 1988. But as the decade gave way to the 1990s, the Western surged forward with numerous critically acclaimed and commercially successful films like Kevin Costner's Academy Award–winning picture *Dances with Wolves*, Clint Eastwood's *Unforgiven*, and 1993's *Tombstone*. But as quickly as the genre became viable again, it faded in popularity due to poorly conceived films like *Geronimo*, *Wyatt Earp*, and *Dead Man*.

Following the 1990s and slipping through to the 2000s and into the 2010s, the Western has taken numerous twists and turns as it begins to once again adapt to the tastes of the pop culture–consuming public. The Horror Western and Weird Western genres began to spring up, and filmmaker Taylor Sheridan has proven himself to be a master of the modern Western with his critically acclaimed films *Hell or High Water*, *Wind River*, and the television series *Yellowstone*. As today's audiences have strayed away from going to the movies, the Western has found a new home in the video game realm with the wildly successful *Red Dead Redemption* series of games.

Through all the genre's ups and downs in film and television and from the heights of paperback novels churned out by the likes of Zane Grey and Louis L'Amour, the Western has survived. At the forefront of it all, at the very beginning of mass marketing and entertainment in America, was Buffalo Bill Cody. After appearing as a character in over forty movies, plays, and television programs, Buffalo Bill has remained at the forefront of the entertainment world. President Teddy Roosevelt once said of Buffalo Bill, "[He is an] American of all Americans and his story belongs to the country."[9]

Following his death, Buffalo Bill Cody has become even more iconic throughout the world. So much so that his name graces establishments in remote areas like a saloon in Zimbabwe, Africa, and visitors to Disneyland in Paris can take in two shows a day that represent a revival of Buffalo Bill's Wild West. In fact, there are multiple European comic books printed today featuring Buffalo Bill Cody as the titular hero.[10]

Buffalo Bill's influence does not stop there, however. More than just a character in movies and comic books or the nickname for a professional sports franchise, many credit Cody with popularizing Francis Scott Key's seminal work, "The Star-Spangled Banner." The song was written in 1814 by then thirty-five-year-old lawyer and amateur poet Francis Scott Key after he witnessed the bombardment of Fort McHenry during the Battle of Baltimore, a major engagement during the War of 1812. It is reported that

Buffalo Bill four days before his death

Key saw the large flag with fifteen stripes and fifteen stars waving proudly among the ammunition exploding around it. This scene inspired him to pen the song that soon became America's national anthem.

Buffalo Bill promoted "The Star-Spangled Banner" by having his band play it before most performances, which eventually led to the song being chosen as the country's national anthem. Bill had an even greater influence on popular music during his time in New Orleans, where he eventually encountered Englishman Evelyn Booth, who helped him through his financially catastrophic period in the Crescent City.[11]

During Cody's time in New Orleans, African Americans living in the city began dressing and imitating the Indians in Buffalo Bill's Wild West for the city's large Mardi Gras celebrations. Ceremonial headdresses like the warbonnets worn by Plains tribes in the Wild West were soon mimicked and adorned many of the marchers in the Mardi Gras parades. The songs sung and performed at these parades influenced jazz, rhythm, and blues music, which eventually gave birth to modern-day rock 'n' roll.[12]

While his life's focus was promoting and monetizing his Wild West show, Buffalo Bill also worked hard to promote the settling of the western United States. He saw the West as a tourist destination and a place where settlers could build a homestead and raise their families while farming the land or harvesting the vast mineral wealth in the area. After founding the town of Cody, Wyoming, Buffalo Bill also became a promoter of Yellowstone National Park and was an advocate for preserving the vast wilderness of the American West.[13]

Buffalo Bill was a proponent of rights for American Indians and suffrage for women, and though he spent much of his early life hunting the great beasts, he eventually became a booster for the preservation of the buffalo.[14] Cody saw America as a place where everyone could find land, prosper financially, and achieve happiness. He was someone who thought life was what you made of it. No matter the circumstances presented to an individual, Cody believed that anything could be achieved through hard work and rugged individualism. His life and his legacy are truly symbolic of the West where he lived and eventually died.

When William Cody finally passed, he had been working for the 101 Ranch Wild West show, attempting to revive his career. Hobbled from a life of riding horses and in poor health from drinking and smoking, Buffalo Bill made his way to Colorado to visit his sister May Cody Decker in November 1916. Bill stopped in Glenwood Springs to

Buffalo Bill's grave. Photograph by Louis Charles McClure, circa 1917.

rest in the hot springs and while there was informed by doctors that he was about to die.[15]

After learning the devastating news, Cody continued to Denver in early January 1917 to see his sister and settle his remaining affairs. Buffalo Bill spent his last days visiting with friends, waiting for his family members to arrive, and giving his last interview to *Outdoor Life* magazine. On January 9 Cody requested to be baptized and made a member of the Catholic Church. It was reported Bill was lucid and aware of everything that was happening. At this time, he gave his final instructions for his funeral services and where he wanted to be buried.[16]

On January 10, 1917, the day following his baptism, Cody died. He was just a little more than a month shy of his seventy-first birthday. His cause of death was listed as "uremic poisoning," which at that time was a term used for an undetermined death. His doctors noted that smoking had damaged his heart and years of drinking had taken a toll on his liver. After Buffalo Bill's death, many dignitaries expressed their sorrow at his passing, including King George V, Kaiser Wilhelm II, and President Woodrow Wilson. The assembled council of Oglala Lakota at the Pine Ridge Indian Reservation also expressed their sadness by stating in a letter that "Buffalo Bill [was] a warm and lasting friend."[17]

During his funeral on January 14, twenty-five thousand mourners passed by his casket in the rotunda of the Colorado State Capitol building. The coffin was later brought by a procession to the Denver Elks Lodge Number 17 where thousands more paid their respects. The old scout's body was then taken to Olinger's Mortuary for embalming. Because Bill died in the winter, the ground on Lookout Mountain overlooking Golden, Colorado, the spot he had designated for his final resting place, was frozen solid and would not permit a proper burial. Bill's body lay in state in the mortuary until June 3, 1917, when he was buried with a full Masonic funeral.[18]

Following Bill's burial on Lookout Mountain, there was a great deal of contention about his final resting spot, as many folks in Wyoming, including some of his own family members, thought Bill should have been buried in Cody, the town the old scout had founded. Unfortunately for those folks, Buffalo Bill had authored a new and proven will in 1913 in which he left much of his estate to his wife and relatives and made the request to be buried at the top of the beautiful mountain overlooking Denver and the Great Plains that he loved so well.[19]

William F. Cody on horseback, supposedly his last appearance in 1916

A great number of conspiracy theories about Cody's burial spot have circulated since his death and continue to this day. When Bill's wife, Louisa, and his last surviving child, Irma, passed away, his niece Mary Jester Allen tried to have his body removed from Lookout Mountain and reburied in Cody in 1925. Johnny Baker, Bill's foster son and former Wild West show performer, had opened a museum near the grave to honor Buffalo Bill's legacy. Along with Bill's two surviving sisters, May and Julia, Baker fought to keep Bill's body in Colorado.[20]

Because of this fight, conspiracy stories began circulating, started by Jester Allen, that Louisa had taken a bribe to bury Bill in Colorado, which was later debunked. She also started making threats that she and her followers were going to steal Cody's corpse and take it back to Wyoming. At this, Johnny Baker reburied Bill and Louisa, who had been laid to rest alongside the old scout, beneath twelve feet of reinforced concrete.[21]

During the late 1920s a caretaker at the museum spread a rumor that some people from Wyoming were going to steal Buffalo Bill's body, but that ended up being just a rumor and the caretaker was reprimanded for it. In 1948, however, the Cody American Legion Post offered a $10,000 reward to anyone who would travel to Colorado, dig up Bill's body, and haul it back to Wyoming. The Colorado National Guard was called into action and stationed around the burial site to protect against the grave robbers.[22]

Then, in the 1990s a tall tale surfaced reporting that Bill's body had been replaced with a vagrant's while it was on ice awaiting burial in Olinger's Mortuary. It was claimed that the corpse was taken to Wyoming and placed in an unmarked grave in the town of Cody. This speculation has been dispelled, however, as it has been noted that on the day of Bill's burial Louisa ordered there to be an open casket. Because of this, literally dozens of people who knew Cody their entire lives would have recognized the imposter, including his wife.[23]

Through all the controversies surrounding his death and subsequent burial, through his highs and lows of popularity, and through his many avenues of influence on American popular culture, William Frederick "Buffalo Bill" Cody remains a fascinating figure. Whether it is his nickname being used by a football franchise in America's most popular professional sports league, through the numerous institutions that bear his name and see millions of visitors every year, or as a character in a piece of popular entertainment like Larry McMurtry's 2015 *New York Times* best-selling book, *The Last Kind Words Saloon*, Buffalo Bill is one of America's favorite sons and symbolic of the spirit of the West. Even with his passing, Cody has remained a legend in popular culture and an individual whose legacy will continue to stand the test of time.

NOTES

CHAPTER 1

1   Eric V. Sorg, *Buffalo Bill: Myth & Reality* (Santa Fe, NM: Ancient City Press, 1988), 26.

2   "Grave of Buffalo Bill's Promoter Will Finally Get Headstone," *Billings Gazette*, April 12, 2017.

3   Ibid.

4   Trav S.D., "P.T. Barnum and the Indians," travsd.wordpress. com, accessed September 15, 2018, https://travsd.wordpress. com/2013/11/18/p-t-barnum-and-the-indians/.

5   Edward Leo Lyman, "Southern Paiute Relations with Their Early Dixie Mormon Neighbors," library.dixie.edu, accessed September 15, 2018, https://library.dixie. edu/special_collections/Juanita_Brooks_lectures/2010.pdf.

6   Susan Shelby Magoffin, edited by Stella M. Drumm, *Down the Santa Fe Trail and into Mexico: The Diary of Susan Shelby Magoffin, 1846–1847* (Lincoln: University of Nebraska Press, 1962), 8.

7   S.D., "P.T. Barnum and the Indians."

8   Ibid.

9   Deanne Stillman, *Blood Brothers: The Story of the Strange Friendship between Sitting Bull and Buffalo Bill* (New York: Simon and Schuster, 2017), 1–2.

10   Ibid.

11   Ibid.

12   Darice Bailer, "The View From/Bridgeport; Museum Invites Visitors to Step Right Up," *New York Times*, January 21, 2001, 14.

13   S.D., "P.T. Barnum and the Indians."

14   A. H. Saxon, *P.T. Barnum: The Man and the Legend* (New York: Columbia University Press, 1989), 100.

15   Ibid.

16   Ibid.

17   Ibid.

18   *Times* staff, "Disastrous Fire," *New York Times*, July 14, 1865, accessed October 10, 2018, https://timesmachine.nytimes.com/timesmachine/1865/07/14/78745435.pdf.

19   Raab Collection, "P.T. Barnum Signed Letter Indian Life Zuni Native Americans," raabcollection.com, accessed October 10, 2018, https://www.raabcollection.com/american-history-autographs/barnum-als-card.

20   S.D., "P.T. Barnum and the Indians."

21   Martyn Lyons, *Books: A Living History* (London: Thames & Hudson, 2013), 156.

22   Shelley Streeby, *American Sensations: Class, Empire, and the Production of Popular Culture*, 2nd ed. (Berkeley: University of California Press, 2002), 3.

CHAPTER 2

1   Alexander Majors, edited by Prentiss Ingraham, *Seventy Years on the Frontier: Alexander Majors' Memoirs of a Lifetime on the Border* (Columbus, OH: Long's College Book Co., 1950), 176.

2   "Historical Notes," ponyexpress.org, accessed January 19, 2019, http://ponyexpress.org/historical-notes/.

3   Louis S. Warren, *Buffalo Bill's America: William Cody and the Wild West Show* (New York: Alfred A. Knopf, 2005), 8–12.

4   Ibid.

5   Robert A. Carter, *Buffalo Bill Cody: The Man Behind the Legend* (New York: John Wiley and Sons, 2002), 512.

6   Warren, *Buffalo Bill's America*, 3.

7   Majors, *Seventy Years on the Frontier*, 176.

8   Ibid., 177.

9   Ibid.

10   Ibid.

11   Stillman, *Blood Brothers*, 42.

12   Ibid., 45.

13   Carter, *Buffalo Bill Cody*, 512.

14   Warren, *Buffalo Bill's America*, 109.

15   Ibid., 90.

16   Ibid.

17   Ibid., 110.

18   Ibid.

19   Ibid., 111.

20   Ibid.

21   Ibid.

22   Ibid.

23   "Battle of Summit Springs, Colorado," legendsofamerica.com, accessed February 2, 2019, https://www.legendsofamerica.com/battle-summit-springs-colorado/.

24   Warren, *Buffalo Bill's America*, 112.

25   Ibid.

26   Ibid., 118.

27   Ibid.

28   Ibid.

29   Ibid., 119.

30   Ibid.

31   Ibid.

32   Ibid.

33   Ibid.

34   Ibid.

35   Sandra K. Sagala, *Buffalo Bill on Stage* (Albuquerque: University of New Mexico Press, 2008), 83–85.

36   "Buffalo Bill's Skirmish at Warbonnet Creek," historynet.com, *American History Magazine,* June 12, 2006, accessed February 5, 2019, https://www.historynet.com/buffalo-bills-skirmish-at-warbonnet-creek.htm.

CHAPTER 3

1   Stuart B. McIver, *Dreamers, Schemers and Scalawags: The Florida Chronicles, Volume 1* (Sarasota, FL: Pineapple Press, 1998), 3–8.

2   Ibid.

3   Ibid.

4   Streeby, *American Sensations*, 3.

5   Tim DeForest, *Storytelling in the Pulps, Comics, and Radio: How Technology Changed Popular Fiction in America* (Jefferson, NC: McFarland Publishing, 2004), 17.

6   Sagala, *Buffalo Bill on Stage*, 8.

7   Ibid.

8   Ibid.

9   Ibid., 21.

10   Ibid., 22.

11   Ibid.

12   Ibid., 3.

13   Warren, *Buffalo Bill's America*, 77.

14   Joy Kasson, *Buffalo Bill's Wild West: Celebrity, Memory, and Popular History* (New York: Hill and Wang, 2000), 45.

15   Ibid.

16   Ibid.

17   Ibid., 46.

18   "Major John M. Burke ('Arizona John')," codyarchive.org, accessed March 11, 2019, http://codyarchive.org/texts/wfc.nsp11554.html.

19   Kasson, *Buffalo Bill's Wild West*, 45–46.

20   Warren, *Buffalo Bill's America*, 158.

21   Ibid.

22   Darlis A. Miller, "Captain Jack Crawford: A Western Military Scout on the Chautauqua Circuit," *South Dakota History* 21, no. 3, 1991: 236–37.

23   Warren, *Buffalo Bill's America*, 158.

24   "Col. Prentiss Ingraham," *Port Gibson Reveille*, August 4, 1905, accessed March 13, 2019, https://chroniclingamerica.loc.gov/lccn/sn86090233/1904-08-25/ed-1/seq-1/.

25   "Ingraham, Prentiss," ulib.niu.edu, accessed March 13, 2019, https://www.ulib.niu.edu/badndp/ingraham_prentiss.html.

26   Ibid.

27   Kasson, *Buffalo Bill's Wild West*, 241.

28   "Ingraham, Prentiss," ulib.niu.edu.

29   John Koster, "Nate Salsbury Helped Buffalo Bill Become the World's Top Showman," history.net, accessed March 13, 2019, https://www.historynet.com/nate-salsbury-helped-buffalo-bill-become-worlds-top-showman.htm.

30   Ibid.

31   Sandra K. Sagala, "Buffalo Bill Cody v. Doc Carver: The Battle of the Wild West," *Nebraska History*, 2004, 4.

32   Warren, *Buffalo Bill's America*, 220.

33   Ibid.

CHAPTER 4

1   Sagala, "Cody v. Carver," 4.

2   Ibid.

3   Ibid., 5.

4   "A Grand Success," *Omaha Bee*, May 21, 1883.

5   Sagala, "Cody v. Carver," 5.

6   Ibid., 6.

7   "Capt. Bogardus History," targetballs.com, accessed March 16, 2019, http://www.targetballs.com/storyVault_3.php.

8   Sagala, "Cody v. Carver," 6.

9   Ibid., 3–7.

10   Ibid.

11   Ibid., 7.

12   Ibid.

13   Ibid., 7–8.

14   Ibid., 8.

15   Ibid.

16   Ibid.

17   Ibid., 9.

18   Ibid.

19   Ibid., 9–10.

20   Ibid., 11.

21   Ibid., 12.

22   Ibid.

23   Ibid.

24   Ibid., 13.

25   Ibid.

26   Ibid.

27   Ibid., 14.

28   Ibid.

29   Ibid.

30   Ibid.

31   Ibid., 5.

CHAPTER 5

1   "Ingraham, Prentiss," ulib.niu.edu.

2   Kasson, *Buffalo Bill's Wild West*, 25.

3   Ibid., 26–27.

4   Ibid.

5   Ibid.

6   Ibid.

7   Lyons, *Books*, 156.

8   "Buffalo Bill Dime Novels," brandeisspecialcollections.blogspot.com, June 4, 2014, accessed April 1, 2019, http://brandeisspecialcollections.blogspot.com/2014/06/buffalo-bill-dime-novels.html.

9   Ibid.

10   Brian Cronin, "Comic Book Questions Answered: What Was the First Variant Cover?" cbr.com, April 24, 2008, accessed March 30, 2019, https://www.cbr.com/comic-book-questions-answered-what-was-the-first-variant-cover/.

11   Lyons, *Books*, 156.

12   Ed Hulse, *The Blood 'n' Thunder Guide to Collecting Pulps* (Morris Plains, NJ: Murania Press, 2009), 137–41.

13   Kasson, *Buffalo Bill's Wild West*, 109–10.

14   Ibid., 107.

15   Ibid., 117–19.

16   Lyons, *Books*, 156.

17   Lyons, *Books*, 156.

18   Ibid.

19   Ibid.

20   "Buffalo Bill: An American Bison Hunter and Showman Best Known for His Portrayal of the Wild West," comicvine.gamespot.com, accessed April 6, 2019, https://comicvine.gamespot.com/buffalo-bill/4005-1838/.

21   Ibid.

CHAPTER 6

1   "John Nelson," codyarchive.org, accessed June 8, 2019, http://codyarchive.org/life/wfc.person.html#nelson.j.

2   Ibid.

3   Ibid.

4   Ibid.

5   Stillman, *Blood Brothers*, 20.

6   Ibid.

7   "John Nelson," codyarchive.org.

8   "Was Annie a Real Western Girl?" webarchive.org, accessed June 14, 2019, https://web.archive.org/web/20021015053658/http://www.ormiston.com/annieoakley/tales.html#KAISER.

9   "Inventing Entertainment: The Early Motion Pictures and Sound Recordings of the Edison Companies," loc.gov, accessed June 14, 2019, https://www.loc.gov/collections/edison-company-motion-pictures-and-sound-recordings/about-this-collection/.

10   Park County Travel Council, "Thirteen Things You Probably Didn't Know about Buffalo Bill," codyyellowstone.org, April 12, 2018, accessed June 15, 2019, https://www.codyyellowstone.org/press/thirteen-things-you-probably-didnt-know-about-buffalo-bill-cody/.

11   Stillman, *Blood Brothers*, 21.

12   Ibid.

13   Ibid., 22.

14   Ibid., 24.

15   Ibid.

16   Ibid., 25.

17   "Biography: Sitting Bull," pbs.org, accessed June 29, 2019, https://www.pbs.org/wgbh/americanexperience/features/oakley-sitting-bull/.

18   Ibid., 183.

19   Stillman, *Blood Brothers*, 182.

20   Ibid.

21   Ibid., xi.

22   Ibid., 224.

23   Ibid., 225.

24   "Johnny Baker," findagrave.com, accessed August 24, 2019, https://www.finda-grave.com/memorial/6186/johnny-baker.

25   "Buffalo Bill's Wild West," codyarchive.org, March 1, 1887, accessed August 24, 2019, http://codyarchive.org/memorabilia/wfc.mem00012.html.

26   Ibid.

27   Ibid.

28   Ibid.

29   Steve Friesen, "Celebrating Buffalo Bill," *True West*, March 2, 2011, accessed August 24, 2019, https://truewestmagazine.com/celebrating-buffalo-bill/.

CHAPTER 7

1   "George Booth, 2nd Earl of Warrington," thepeerage.com, accessed July 22, 2019, http://www.thepeerage.com/p2820.htm#i28200.

2   "Whitehall," *London Gazette*, November 21, 1834, accessed July 22, 2019, https://www.thegazette.co.uk/London/issue/19212/page/2085.

3   "Crown Office," *London Gazette*, February 22, 1916, accessed July 22, 2019, https://www.thegazette.co.uk/London/issue/29483/page/1946.

4   Ibid.

5   [Journal 1884–1885, Box 1, FF1] English Sporting Men's Travel in America Papers, WH121, Western History Collection, Denver Public Library.

6   Evelyn Booth, edited by Kellen Cutsforth, *Buffalo Bill, Boozers, Brothels, and Bare Knuckle Brawlers: An Englishman's Journal of Adventure in America* (Billings, MT: TwoDot, 2015), ix.

7   "Cambridge University Alumni 1261–1900," ancestrylibrary.com, accessed May 5, 2019, http://search.ancestrylibrary.com/cgi-bin/sse.dll?rank=1&new=1& MSAV=1&msT=1&gss=angs-g&gsfn=Reginald+Beaumont+&gsln=Heygate&m srpn__ftp=Cambridge%2c+Cambridgeshire%2c+England&msrpn=82304&ms

rpn_PInfo=8-|0|0|3257|3251|0|0|0|5256|82304|0|&catBucket=rstp&uidh=x14&=r%2c0&_83004003-n_xcl=f&pcat=ROOT_CATEGORY&h=123142&recoff=6+7+8&db=alumni6&indiv=1.

8   "Rasmussen Family Tree," trees.ancestrylibrary.com, accessed November 18, 2019, http://trees.ancestrylibrary.com/tree/6814801/person/-1219358644?ssrc.

9   "Citizens of Portland Credit Mastodon Story," *San Francisco Call*, September 12, 1903, 10.

10   Roger Longrigg, *The History of Horse Racing* (New York: Stein and Day Publishers, 1972), 147–50.

11   "New York Passenger Lists, 1820–1957," ancestrylibrary.com, accessed May 5, 2019, http://search.ancestrylibrary.com/cgi-bin/sse.dll?rank=1&new=1&MSAV=1&msT=1&gss=angs-g&gsfn=Evelyn+&gsln=Booth&msbdy=1860&msddy=1901&msady=1884&msapn__ftp=Sandy+Hook%2c+Monmouth%2c+New+Jersey%2c+USA&msapn=8679&msapn_PInfo=8-%7c0%7c1652393%7c0%7c2%7c3244%7c33%7c0%7c2048%7c8679%7c0%7c&catBucket=rstp&uidh=x14&_83004003-n_xcl=f&pcat=ROOT_CATEGORY&h=10065116&recoff=8+9&db=nypl&indiv=1&ml_rpos=1.

12   Longrigg, *Horse Racing*, 150.

13   *Blackwood's Edinburgh Magazine,* vol. 15, London, 1844, 176.

14   David Parlett, *Oxford Dictionary of Card Games* (Oxford: Oxford University Press, 1996), 16.

15   Ibid.

16   "Faro—Card Game of the Southwest," desertusa.com, accessed September 3, 2019, http://www.desertusa.com/desert-activity/faro-card-game.html.

17   Ibid.

18   Albert H. Morehead, Geoffrey Mott-Smith, and Philip D. Morehead, *Hoyle's Rules of Games,* rev. ed. (New York: Signet Publishing, 2001), 290.

19   "Faro—Card Game of the Southwest," desertusa.com.

20   Ibid.

21   Ibid.

22   Ibid.

23   Richard J. Walsh, *The Making of Buffalo Bill* (Chicago: A.L. Burt and Co., 1928), 240.

24   Donald R. Hickey, Susan A. Wunder, and John R. Wunder, *Nebraska Moments* (Lincoln: University of Nebraska Press, 2007), 108.

25   Glenn D. Bradley, *The Story of the Pony Express: An Account of the Most Remarkable Mail Service Ever in Existence, and Its Place in History* (Chicago: A.C. McClurg & Co., 1913), 69.

26   Kellen Cutsforth, "Boozers, Brothels, Bare-Knuckle Brawlers, and Buffalo Bill's Little-Known Business Partner," *Denver Westerners Roundup,* June 2016, 13.

27   Ibid.

28   Walsh, *The Making of Buffalo Bill,* 240.

29   William F. Cody, *Story of the Wild West and Campfire Chats* (Philadelphia and St. Louis: Historical Publishing Co., 1888), 699.

30   [Memoir, envelope 1] Nate Salsbury Papers, M688, Western History Collection, Denver Public Library.

31   Ibid.

32   "The New Billiard-Player," *New York Times,* September 21, 1875.

33   "Yank Adams, of Chicago," *Omaha Daily Bee,* November 2, 1889, 2.

34   "All Done with the Fingers: The Manner in Which Yank Adams Toys with the Spheres," *The Sun,* June 14, 1891, 16.

35   Ibid.

36   [Journal 1884–1885, Box 1, FF1] English Sporting Men's Travel in America Papers, WH121, Western History Collection, Denver Public Library.

37 "Doc Powell," documentcloud.org, accessed September 5, 2019, https://assets. documentcloud.org/documents/606726/doc-powell.pdf.

38 Ibid.

39 Greg Hoffman, "Doc Powell Had Strong State Ties," onmilwaukee.com, February 15, 2009, accessed September 5, 2019, http://onmilwaukee.com/visitors/ articles/docpowell.html.

40 Ibid.

41 [Journal 1884–1885, Box 1, FF1] English Sporting Men's Travel in America Papers, WH121, Western History Collection, Denver Public Library.

42 Ibid.

43 "Our Monthly Record," *The Outing: An Illustrated Monthly Magazine of Recreation, Volume 6*, April to September, 1885, 378.

44 [Journal 1884–1885, Box 1, FF1] English Sporting Men's Travel in America Papers, WH121, Western History Collection, Denver Public Library.

45 Ibid.

46 Cody, *Story of the Wild West*, 699.

47 [Journal 1884–1885, Box 1, FF1] English Sporting Men's Travel in America Papers, WH121, Western History Collection, Denver Public Library.

48 Cody, *Story of the Wild West*, 699.

49 William F. "Buffalo Bill" Cody Collection, MS 6, Harold McCracken Research Library, Buffalo Bill Historical Center.

50 Ibid.

51 "Wiman, Erastus," biographi.ca, accessed August 13, 2019, http://www.biographi.ca/en/bio/wiman_erastus_13E.html.

52   Kellen Cutsforth, "Evelyn Booth Took a Shot at Fame as a Partner of Buffalo Bill's Wild West: But Cody's English Benefactor Is Largely Forgotten Today," *Wild West*, February 2014, 28–29.

53   Ibid

54   Ibid.

CHAPTER 8

1   Ted Hovett, "America on Display: Constructing and Containing Images of the United States," *Interdisciplinary Studies in the Long Nineteenth Century* 19, November 2009, 9.

2   Steve Friesen, *Buffalo Bill: Scout, Showman, Visionary* (Golden, CO: Fulcrum Publishing, 2010), 66.

3   Warren, *Buffalo Bill's America*, 281–82.

4   Ibid.

5   [Clippings 1886–1887, Box 3, FF37] William Frederick Cody/Buffalo Bill Papers, WH72, Western History Collection, Denver Public Library.

6   Cutsforth, "Boozers, Brothels, Bare-Knuckle Brawlers," 13.

7   [Clippings 1886–1887, Box 3, FF37] William Frederick Cody/Buffalo Bill Papers, WH72, Western History Collection, Denver Public Library.

8   Ibid.

9   Ibid.

10   [Clippings 1887, Box 3, FF38] William Frederick Cody/Buffalo Bill Papers, WH72, Western History Collection, Denver Public Library.

11   Ibid.

12   Ibid.

13   Hovett, "America on Display," 19.

14 Ibid.

15 Friesen, *Scout, Showman, Visionary*, 67.

16 Ibid.

17 Ibid., 70.

18 Ibid., 67.

19 Ibid.

20 Ibid.

21 Ibid.

22 Alan Gallop, *Buffalo Bill's British Wild West* (Gloucestershire, UK: Sutton Publishing, 2001), 129.

23 Friesen, *Scout, Showman, Visionary*, 73.

24 Ibid.

25 Ibid.

26 Kasson, *Buffalo Bill's Wild West*, 83.

27 Ibid.

28 [Clippings 1886–1887, Box 4, FF17] William Frederick Cody/Buffalo Bill Papers, WH72, Western History Collection, Denver Public Library.

29 Kasson, *Buffalo Bill's Wild West*, 83.

30 Ibid., 84.

31 "William 'Buffalo Bill' Cody," wdl.org, accessed May 21, 2019, https://www.wdl.org/en/item/11200/.

32 Leslie Maryann Neal, "What Remains of the 1893 Chicago World's Fair Today," allthatsinteresting.com, June 4, 2014, accessed May 24, 2019, https://allthatsinteresting.com/1893-chicago-worlds-fair.

33   Ibid.

34   Joseph Gustaitis, *Chicago's Greatest Year—1893: The White City and the Birth of a Modern Metropolis* (Carbondale, IL: Southern Illinois Press, 2013), 210–13.

35   JD Crighton and Herman W. Mudgett, MD, *Holmes' Own Story: Confessed 27 Murders, Lied, Then Died* (Murrieta, CA: Aerobear Classics, 2018), 87–90.

36   History.com editors, "Murder Castle," history.com, July 13, 2017, accessed May 25, 2019, https://www.history.com/topics/crime/murder-castle.

37   Allison Hirschlag, "9 Things You Didn't Know about America's First Serial Killer H. H. Holmes," mentalfloss.com, May 16, 2017, accessed May 25, 2019, http://mentalfloss.com/article/72642/9-things-you-didnt-know-about-americas-first-serial-killer-hh-holmes.

38   Lauren M. Barrow, Ron A. Rufo, and Saul Arambula, *Police and Profiling in the United States: Applying Theory to Criminal Investigations* (Boca Raton, FL: CRC Press, 2013), 198.

39   Erik Larson, *The Devil in the White City: Murder, Magic and Madness at the Fair That Changed America* (New York: Crown Publishing Group, 2003), 222.

40   Ibid.

41   Geoffrey Johnson, "'Buffalo Bill' Cody Wowed Chicago with His 'Wild West' Shows," chicagotribune.com, February 23, 2017, accessed May 25, 2019, https://www.chicagotribune.com/opinion/commentary/ct-buffalo-bill-cody-flashback-perspec-0226-md-20170223-story.html.

42   Ibid.

43   Ibid.

44   Charles Eldridge Griffen, *Four Years in Europe with Buffalo Bill* (Lincoln: University of Nebraska Press, 2010), xviii.

45   Karen Bornemann Spies, *Buffalo Bill Cody: Legend of the Wild West* (Berkley Heights, NJ: Enslow Publishing, 2015), 65.

46   Ibid.

47   Chris Enss, *The Many Loves of Buffalo Bill: The True Story of Life on the Wild West Show* (Helena, MT: TwoDot, 2010), 94.

48   Ibid.

49   Ibid., 95–97.

50   Ibid.

51   Allyson Reedy, "A Glimpse into the Life of Buffalo Bill," 5280. com, January 2017, accessed July 26, 2019, https://www.5280. com/2016/12/a-glimpse-into-the-life-of-buffalo-bill/.

52   Juti A. Winchester, "Times to Try a Soul, William F. Cody in 1876, Remembering Kit Carson Cody," *Points West*, Winter 2003, accessed July 30, 2019, https://centerofthewest.org/2017/10/06/points-west-1876-kit-cody/.

53   "Orra Maude Cody," findagrave.com, accessed July 30, 2019, https://www.findagrave.com/memorial/2886/orra-maude-cody.

54   "Arta Lucille Cody," findagrave.com, accessed July 30, 2019, https://www.findagrave.com/memorial/2887/arta-lucille-cody.

55   Carter, *Buffalo Bill Cody*, 65.

56   Ibid.

57   Kasson, *Buffalo Bill's Wild West*, 144.

58   Ibid.

59   Ibid., 146.

60   Ibid., 147.

61   Ibid., 148.

62   Ibid.

63   Ibid., 151.

64   Ibid., 152–54.

65   Ibid.

66   Ibid., 154.

67   Ibid., 155.

68   Friesen, *Scout, Showman, Visionary*, 138.

69   Ibid.

70   Ibid.

71   Kasson, *Buffalo Bill's Wild West*, 155.

CHAPTER 9

1   Friesen, *Scout, Showman, Visionary*, 136.

2   "#32 Buffalo Bills," forbes.com, accessed July 20, 2019, https://www.forbes.com/teams/buffalo-bills/#7e1cc1d9625d.

3   "Franchise Nicknames," profootballhof.com, accessed October 1, 2019, https://www.profootballhof.com/news/franchise-nicknames/.

4   Ibid.

5   "Buckhorn Exchange," atlasobscura.com, accessed September 27, 2019, https://www.atlasobscura.com/places/buckhorn-exchange.

6   "The Life and Legacy of Buffalo Bill," treasurestatelifestyles.com, accessed July 21, 2019, http://treasurestatelifestyles.com/the-life-and-legacy-of-buffalo-bill/.

7   Norman O. Keim, *Our Movie Houses: A History of Film & Cinematic Innovation in Central New York* (Syracuse, NY: Syracuse University Press, 2008), 17.

8   John Hemphill, "The Decline of the Western and the Continuing Resonance of *The Ballad of Little Jo*," talkhouse.com, accessed September 21, 2019, https://www.talkhouse.com/the-decline-of-the-western-and-the-continuing-resonance-of-the-ballad-of-little-jo/.

9   Friesen, *Scout, Showman, Visionary*, 155.

10   Ibid.

11   Ibid.

12   Ibid., 155–56.

13   Ibid., 156.

14   Ibid.

15   Ibid., 141.

16   Ibid., 141–42.

17   Ibid.

18   Ibid., 145.

19   Ibid.

20   Ibid., 148.

21   Ibid., 150.

22   Ibid.

23   Ibid., 150–51.

BIBLIOGRAPHY

MANUSCRIPTS AND PRIMARY RESOURCES

English Sporting Men's Travel in America Papers, WH121, Western History Collection, Denver Public Library.

Nate Salsbury Papers, M688, Western History Collection, Denver Public Library.

William F. "Buffalo Bill" Cody Collection, MS 6, Harold McCracken Research Library, Buffalo Bill Historical Center.

William Frederick Cody/Buffalo Bill Papers, WH72, Western History Collection, Denver Public Library.

BOOKS

Barrow, Lauren M., Ron A. Rufo, and Saul Arambula. *Police and Profiling in the United States: Applying Theory to Criminal Investigations*. Boca Raton, FL: CRC Press, 2013.

Booth, Evelyn, edited by Kellen Cutsforth. *Buffalo Bill, Boozers, Brothels, and Bare Knuckle Brawlers: An Englishman's Journal of Adventure in America*. Billings, MT: TwoDot, 2015.

Bradley, Glenn D. *The Story of the Pony Express: An Account of the Most Remarkable Mail Service Ever in Existence and Its Place in History*. Chicago: A.C. McClurg & Co., 1913.

Carter, Robert A. *Buffalo Bill Cody: The Man Behind the Legend*. New York: John Wiley and Sons, 2002.

Cody, William F. *Story of the Wild West and Campfire Chats*. Philadelphia and St. Louis, MO: Historical Publishing Co., 1888.

Crighton, JD, and Herman W. Mudgett, MD. *Holmes' Own Story: Confessed 27 Murders, Lied, Then Died*. Murrieta, CA: Aerobear Classics, 2018.

DeForest, Tim. *Storytelling in the Pulps, Comics, and Radio: How Technology Changed Popular Fiction in America*. Jefferson, NC: McFarland Publishing, 2004.

Enss, Chris. *The Many Loves of Buffalo Bill: The True Story of Life on the Wild West Show*. Helena, MT: TwoDot, 2010.

Friesen, Steve. *Buffalo Bill: Scout, Showman, Visionary*. Golden, CO: Fulcrum Publishing, 2010.

Gallop, Alan. *Buffalo Bill's British Wild West*. Gloucestershire, UK: Sutton Publishing, 2001.

Griffen, Charles Eldridge. *Four Years in Europe with Buffalo Bill*. Lincoln: University of Nebraska Press, 2010.

Gustaitis, Joseph. *Chicago's Greatest Year—1893: The White City and the Birth of a Modern Metropolis*. Carbondale, IL: Southern Illinois Press, 2013.

Hickey, Donald R., Susan A. Wunder, and John R. Wunder. *Nebraska Moments*. Lincoln: University of Nebraska Press, 2007.

Hulse, Ed. *The Blood 'n' Thunder Guide to Collecting Pulps*. Morris Plains, NJ: Murania Press, 2009.

Kasson, Joy. *Buffalo Bill's Wild West: Celebrity, Memory, and Popular History*. New York: Hill and Wang, 2000.

Keim, Norman O. *Our Movie Houses: A History of Film & Cinematic Innovation in Central New York*. Syracuse, NY: Syracuse University Press, 2008.

Larson, Erik. *The Devil in the White City: Murder, Magic and Madness at the Fair That Changed America*, New York: Crown Publishing Group, 2003.

Longrigg, Roger. *The History of Horse Racing*. New York: Stein and Day Publishers, 1972.

Lyons, Martyn. *Books: A Living History*. London: Thames & Hudson, 2013.

Magoffin, Susan Shelby, edited by Stella M. Drumm. *Down the Santa Fe Trail and into Mexico: The Diary of Susan Shelby Magoffin, 1846–1847*. Lincoln: University of Nebraska Press, 1962.

Majors, Alexander, edited by Prentiss Ingraham. *Seventy Years on the Frontier: Alexander Majors' Memoirs of a Lifetime on the Border.* Columbus, OH: Long's College Book Co., 1950.

McIver, Stuart B. *Dreamers, Schemers and Scalawags: The Florida Chronicles, Volume 1.* Sarasota, FL: Pineapple Press, 1998.

Morehead, Albert H., Geoffrey Mott-Smith, and Philip D. Morehead. *Hoyle's Rules of Games,* rev. ed. New York: Signet Publishing, 2001.

Parlett, David. *Oxford Dictionary of Card Games.* Oxford, UK: Oxford University Press, 1996.

Sagala, Sandra K. *Buffalo Bill on Stage.* Albuquerque: University of New Mexico Press, 2008.

Saxon, A. H. *P. T. Barnum: The Man and the Legend.* New York: Columbia University, 1989.

Sorg, Eric V. *Buffalo Bill: Myth & Reality.* Santa Fe, NM: Ancient City, 1988

Spies, Karen Bornemann. *Buffalo Bill Cody: Legend of the Wild West.* Berkley Heights, NJ: Enslow Publishing, 2015.

Stillman, Deanne. *Blood Brothers: The Story of the Strange Friendship between Sitting Bull and Buffalo Bill.* New York: Simon and Schuster, 2017.

Streeby, Shelley. *American Sensations: Class, Empire, and the Production of Popular Culture,* 2nd ed. Berkeley: University of California Press, 2002.

Walsh, Richard J. *The Making of Buffalo Bill.* Chicago: A.L. Burt and Co., 1928.

Warren, Louis S. *Buffalo Bill's America: William Cody and the Wild West Show.* New York: Alfred A. Knopf, 2005.

PERIODICALS

Bailer, Darice. "The View From/Bridgeport; Museum Invites Visitors to Step Right Up." *New York Times,* January 21, 2001, 14.

Billings Gazette. "Grave of Buffalo Bill's Promoter Will Finally Get Headstone." April 12, 2017.

Blackwood's Edinburgh Magazine, vol. 15. Pamphlet. London, 1844, 176.

Cutsforth, Kellen. "Boozers, Brothels, Bare-Knuckle Brawlers, and Buffalo Bill's Little-Known Business Partner." *Denver Westerners Roundup,* June 2016, 13.

Cutsforth, Kellen. "Evelyn Booth Took a Shot at Fame as a Partner of Buffalo Bill's Wild West: But Cody's English Benefactor Is Largely Forgotten Today." *Wild West*, February 2014, 26.

Hovett, Ted. "America on Display: Constructing and Containing Images of the United States." *Interdisciplinary Studies in the Long Nineteenth Century* 19, November 2009, 9.

Miller, Darlis A. "Captain Jack Crawford: A Western Military Scout on the Chautauqua Circuit." *South Dakota History* 21, no. 3, 1991, 236–37.

New York Times. "The New Billiard-Player." September 21, 1875.

Omaha Bee. "A Grand Success." May 21, 1883.

Omaha Daily Bee. "Yank Adams, of Chicago." November 2, 1889, 2.

The Outing: An Illustrated Monthly Magazine of Recreation, Volume 6. "Our Monthly Record." April to September 1885, 378.

Sagala, Sandra K. "Buffalo Bill Cody v. Doc Carver: The Battle of the Wild West." *Nebraska History*, 2004, 4.

San Francisco Call. "Citizens of Portland Credit Mastodon Story." September 12, 1903, 10.

The Sun. "All Done with the Fingers: The Manner in Which Yank Adams Toys with the Spheres." June 14, 1891, 16.

INTERNET RESOURCES

"#32 Buffalo Bills." Forbes.com. Accessed July 20, 2019. https://www.forbes.com/teams/buffalo-bills/#7e1cc1d9625d.

"Arta Lucille Cody." Findagrave.com. Accessed July 30, 2019. https://www.findagrave.com/memorial/2887/arta-lucille-cody.

"Battle of Summit Springs, Colorado." Legendsofamerica.com. Accessed February 2, 2019. https://www.legendsofamerica.com/battle-summit-springs-colorado/.

"Biography: Sitting Bull." Pbs.org. Accessed June 29, 2019. https://www.pbs.org/wgbh/americanexperience/features/oakley-sitting-bull/.

"Buckhorn Exchange." Atlasobscura.com. Accessed September 27, 2019. https://www.atlasobscura.com/places/buckhorn-exchange.

"Buffalo Bill: An American Bison Hunter and Showman Best Known for His Portrayal of the Wild West." Comicvine.gamespot.com. Accessed April 6, 2019. https://comicvine.gamespot.com/buffalo-bill/4005-1838/.

"Buffalo Bill Dime Novels." Brandeisspecialcollections.blogspot.com, June 4, 2014. Accessed April 1, 2019. http://brandeisspecialcollections.blogspot.com/2014/06/buffalo-bill-dime-novels.html.

"Buffalo Bill's Skirmish at Warbonnet Creek." Historynet.com. *American History Magazine*, June 12, 2006. Accessed February 5, 2019. https://www.historynet.com/buffalo-bills-skirmish-at-warbonnet-creek.htm.

"Buffalo Bill's Wild West." Codyarchive.org, March 1, 1887. Accessed August 24, 2019. http://codyarchive.org/memorabilia/wfc.mem00012.html.

"Cambridge University Alumni 1261–1900." Ancestrylibrary.com. Accessed May 5, 2019. http://search.ancestrylibrary.com/cgi-bin/sse.dll?rank=1&new=1&MSAV=1&msT=1&gss=angs-g&gsfn=Reginald+Beaumont+&gsln=Heygate&msrpn__ftp=Cambridge%2c+Cambridgeshire%2c+England&msrpn=82304&msrpn_PInfo=8-|0|0|3257|3251|0|0|0|5256|82304|0|&catBucket=rstp&uidh=x14&=r%2c0&_83004003-n_xcl=f&pcat=ROOT_CATEGORY&h=123142&recoff=6+7+8&db=alumni6&indiv=1.

"Capt. Bogardus History." Targetballs.com. Accessed March 16, 2019. http://www.targetballs.com/storyVault_3.php.

"Col. Prentiss Ingraham." *Port Gibson Reveille*, August 4, 1905. Accessed March 13, 2019. https://chroniclingamerica.loc.gov/lccn/sn86090233/1904-08-25/ed-1/seq-1/.

Cronin, Brian. "Comic Book Questions Answered: What Was the First Variant Cover?" Cbr.com, April 24, 2008. Accessed March 30, 2019. https://www.cbr.com/comic-book-questions-answered-what-was-the-first-variant-cover/.

"Crown Office." *London Gazette*, February 22, 1916. Accessed July 22, 2019. https://www.thegazette.co.uk/London/issue/29483/page/1946.

"Doc Powell." Documentcloud.org. Accessed September 5, 2019. https://assets.documentcloud.org/documents/606726/doc-powell.pdf.

"Faro—Card Game of the Southwest." Desertusa.com. Accessed September 3, 2019. http://www.desertusa.com/desert-activity/faro-card-game.html.

"Franchise Nicknames." Profootballhof.com. Accessed October 1, 2019. https://www.profootballhof.com/news/franchise-nicknames/.

Friesen, Steve. "Celebrating Buffalo Bill." *True West*, March 2, 2011. Accessed August 24, 2019. https://truewestmagazine.com/celebrating-buffalo-bill/.

"George Booth, 2nd Earl of Warrington." Thepeerage.com. Accessed July 22, 2019. http://www.thepeerage.com/p2820.htm#i28200.

Hemphill, John. "The Decline of the Western and the Continuing Resonance of *The Ballad of Little Jo*." Talkhouse.com. Accessed September 21, 2019. https://www .talkhouse.com/the-decline-of-the-western-and-the-continuing-resonance-of -the-ballad-of-little-jo/.

Hirschlag, Allison. "9 Things You Didn't Know about America's First Serial Killer H. H. Holmes." Mentalfloss.com, May 16, 2017. Accessed May 25, 2019. http:// mentalfloss.com/article/72642/9-things-you-didnt-know-about-americas-first -serial-killer-hh-holmes.

"Historical Notes." Ponyexpress.org. Accessed January 19, 2019. http://ponyexpress .org/historical-notes/.

History.com editors. "Murder Castle." History.com, July 13, 2017. Accessed May 25, 2019. https://www.history.com/topics/crime/murder-castle.

Hoffman, Greg. "Doc Powell Had Strong State Ties." Onmilwaukee.com, February 15, 2009. Accessed September 5, 2019. http://onmilwaukee.com/ visitors/articles/docpowell.html.

"Ingraham, Prentiss." Ulib.niu.edu. Accessed March 13, 2019. https://www.ulib.niu .edu/badndp/ingraham_prentiss.html.

"Inventing Entertainment: The Early Motion Pictures and Sound Recordings of the Edison Companies." Loc.gov. Accessed June 14, 2019. https://www.loc.gov/ collections/edison-company-motion-pictures-and-sound-recordings/about-this -collection/.

"John Nelson." Codyarchive.org. Accessed June 8, 2019. http://codyarchive.org/ life/wfc.person.html#nelson.j.

"Johnny Baker." Findagrave.com. Accessed August 24, 2019. https://www.findagrave .com/memorial/6186/johnny-baker.

Johnson, Geoffrey. "'Buffalo Bill' Cody Wowed Chicago with His 'Wild West' Shows." Chicagotribune.com, February 23, 2017. Accessed May 25, 2019. https://www.chicagotribune.com/opinion/commentary/ct-buffalo-bill-cody -flashback-perspec-0226-md-20170223-story.html.

Koster, John. "Nate Salsbury Helped Buffalo Bill Become the World's Top Showman." History.net, accessed March 13, 2019. https://www.historynet.com/nate-salsbury-helped-buffalo-bill-become-worlds-top-showman.htm.

"The Life and Legacy of Buffalo Bill." Treasurestatelifestyles.com. Accessed July 21, 2019. http://treasurestatelifestyles.com/the-life-and-legacy-of-buffalo-bill/.

Lyman, Edward Leo. "Southern Paiute Relations with Their Early Dixie Mormon Neighbors." Library.dixie.edu. Accessed September 15, 2019. https://library.dixie.edu/special_collections/Juanita_Brooks_lectures/2010.pdf.

"Major John M. Burke ('Arizona John')." Codyarchive.org. Accessed March 11, 2019. http://codyarchive.org/texts/wfc.nsp11554.html.

Neal, Leslie Maryann. "What Remains of the 1893 Chicago World's Fair Today." Allthatsinteresting.com, June 4, 2014. Accessed May 24, 2019. https://allthatsinteresting.com/1893-chicago-worlds-fair.

"New York Passenger Lists, 1820–1957." Ancestrylibrary.com. Accessed May 5, 2019. http://search.ancestrylibrary.com/cgi-bin/sse.dll?rank=1&new=1&MSAV=1&msT=1&gss=angs-g&gsfn=Evelyn+&gsln=Booth&msbdy=1860&msddy=1901&msady=1884&msapn__ftp=Sandy+Hook%2c+Monmouth%2c+New+Jersey%2c+USA&msapn=8679&msapn_PInfo=8-%7c0%7c1652393%7c0%7c2%7c3244%7c33%7c0%7c2048%7c8679%7c0%7c&catBucket=rstp&uidh=x14&_83004003-n_xcl=f&pcat=ROOT_CATEGORY&h=10065116&recoff=8+9&db=nypl&indiv=1&ml_rpos=1.

"Orra Maude Cody." Findagrave.com. Accessed July 30, 2019. https://www.findagrave.com/memorial/2886/orra-maude-cody.

Park County Travel Council. "Thirteen Things You Probably Didn't Know about Buffalo Bill." Codyyellowstone.org, April 12, 2018. Accessed June 15, 2019. https://www.codyyellowstone.org/press/thirteen-things-you-probably-didnt-know-about-buffalo-bill-cody/.

Raab Collection. "P. T. Barnum Signed Letter Indian Life Zuni Native Americans." Raabcollection.com. Accessed October 10, 2018. https://www.raabcollection.com/american-history-autographs/barnum-als-card.

"Rasmussen Family Tree." Trees.ancestrylibrary.com. Accessed November 18, 2019. http://trees.ancestrylibrary.com/tree/6814801/person/-1219358644?ssrc.

Reedy, Allyson. "A Glimpse into the Life of Buffalo Bill." 5280.com, January 2017. Accessed July 26, 2019. https://www.5280.com/2016/12/a-glimpse-into-the -life-of-buffalo-bill/.

S. D. , Trav. "P. T. Barnum and the Indians." Travsd.wordpress.com. Accessed September 15, 2018. https://travsd.wordpress.com/2013/11/18/p-t-barnum -and-the-indians/.

Times staff. "Disastrous Fire." *New York Times*, July 14, 1865. Accessed October 10, 2018. https://timesmachine.nytimes.com/timesmachine/ 1865/07/14/78745435.pdf.

"Was Annie a Real Western Girl?" Webarchive.org. Accessed June 14, 2019. https://web.archive.org/web/20021015053658/http://www.ormiston.com/ annieoakley/tales.html#KAISER.

"Whitehall." *London Gazette*, November 21, 1834. Accessed July 22, 2019. https:// www.thegazette.co.uk/London/issue/19212/page/2085.

"William 'Buffalo Bill' Cody." Wdl.org. Accessed May 21, 2019. https://www.wdl .org/en/item/11200/.

"Wiman, Erastus." Biographi.ca. Accessed August 13, 2019. http://www.biographi .ca/en/bio/wiman_erastus_13E.html.

Winchester, Juti A. "Times to Try a Soul, William F. Cody in 1876, Remembering Kit Carson Cody." *Points West*, Winter 2003. Accessed July 30, 2019. https:// centerofthewest.org/2017/10/06/points-west-1876-kit-cody/.

INDEX

(Note: Illustration page references are in *italics*.)

Adams, Frank B. "Yank," 98, 99

African Americans, 120, 137

Alexis, Grand Duke, 34

Allen, Mary Jester, 141

American Exhibition, 100, 103, 105–108

American Indians, *5*, 8, 125
 in Buffalo Bill's Wild West, 1, 11, *25*
 Cody's belief in rights for, 137
 early interactions with traders and
  mountain men, 8
 exploitation by P. T. Barnum, 11–13
 in London, 105, 107

American Museum, 11–12

Archer, Frederick J., 92

Bailey, James A., *119*, 120, 122

Baker, Lewis H. "Johnny," 81–83, *82*, 118,
 124, 141

Barnum, P. T., 11–13, *13*, 14, 43, 120

Beadle's Dime Novels, 60, 63

Black America show, 120

Bogardus, Adam H., 14, 45, *46*, 83, 97

Booth, Evelyn, 87–89, *88*, 92, 95, 98, 99,
 100, 103, 137

Breuil, James, 130

Buckhorn Exchange, 130–131

buffalo, 21, *22*, 137

Buffalo Bill. *See* Cody, Buffalo Bill
 (William F.)

Buffalo Bill, King of the Border Men
 (Buntline), 15, 32

Buffalo Bill and the Indians (film), *132*,
 133, 135

Buffalo Bill Border Stories, 68

Buffalo Bill look-alike contest, 130–131

Buffalo Bill Memorial Museum, 83, 141

Buffalo Bill Stories, 68, *69*, 71

Buffalo Bill's Combination, 34–36, 118

Buffalo Bills football team, 130

Buffalo Bill's Wild West (and Congress of
 Rough Riders of the World), vii, 7. *See
 also* Cody, Buffalo Bill (William F.)
 acrobats, *121*
 at American Exhibition, 103, 105–108
 and American Indians, 5, 11, *25*
 Americans' vision of Old West, 131
 Cody's first ideas about, 39

and Columbian Exposition, 112–116
cowgirls, *114*
and Doc Carver, 43–52
in England, *74,* 100–102, 103, 108
in Europe, *101, 109,* 111–112, 124, *134*
historical reenactments, *4, 6, 10,* 14, 21, *22,* 24, 28, 73, *128, 129*
horsemanship, 73, 112, *114*
and James Bailey, 120
musicians, *134,* 137
in New Orleans, 96–100
in New York City, *104*
parades, 6, *104*
performers and cast, 35–36, 73–86, *85*
and the Pony Express, 21
poster, *110, 113*
promotional techniques, vii, 6, 8, 36
recorded by Thomas Edison, 78
salaries of performers, 79
souvenir programs, 68
on Staten Island, 100
what the shows were like, 6
winter of 1884, 95–96
Buntline, Ned, 15, 31–32, *33,* 34, 36, 58, 60, 125
Burke, Arizona John, 8, 35–36, *37,* 79, 111
Butler, Frank, 76, 78
Byrne, John, 65

Carr, Eugene, 23–24, 79
Carver, William Frank "Doc," 14, 41, 43–52, *44, 46, 51*
  litigation against Buffalo Bill, 48–50
Carver and Crawford's Wild West, 47
Catlin, George, 11
celebrity journalism, 38

Charley (Buffalo Bill's horse), *2,* 108
Cheyenne Indians, 8, 23–24, 26, 28
Chicago, 112–116
Cleveland, Grover, 111
Cody, Buffalo Bill (William F.), *33, 117, 136, 140. See also* Buffalo Bill's Wild West (and Congress of Rough Riders of the World)
  as America's first celebrity, vii, 6, 124, 130
  and Arizona John Burke, 36
  baptism of, 139
  beginning of Wild West show, 45
  Black America show, 120
  as buffalo hunter, 6, 21, *22,* 50
  and Captain Jack Crawford, 36, 38
  changes name of show, 112
  and Charley (horse), *2,* 108
  children, 81, *117,* 118, 120
  and Columbian Exposition, 112–116
  in comic books, 70, 135
  conspiracy theories about burial place, 141
  contrast with P. T. Barnum, 14
  death of, 124, 139
  and dime novels, 39, 55–72
  divorce, 116, 118, 120
  and Doc Carver, 41, 43–52
  in Europe, 111–112, 116, 124
  and Evelyn Booth, 95, 98, 99
  family, *117*
  as film producer, 130
  financial problems, 87–102, 120, 122–123
  as first American hero, 53–72
  and Frank Powell, 98–99
  friendship with Sitting Bull, 79–81, *80*

as frontiersman, *18*

ghost-written novels, 39, 58

and Gordon Lillie, 122–123

grave, *138*

growth of reputation, 15

impact on popular culture, 131, 141–142

and Indian Wars, 23–24, 26–28, 50

influence on popular music, 137

Ingraham acts as press agent for, 47

inspiration sources, 14, 15

as international sensation, 111

and James Bailey, 120, 122

and Johnny Baker, 81–83

on lecture circuit, 123

legacy of, viii, 127–142

litigation against Doc Carver, 48–50

in London, 105–108

military honors, 24

as military scout, 6, 21, 28–29

and movie industry, 130–133, 135

and Nate Salsbury, 39–41, 47

and Ned Buntline, 15, 31–32, 34

in New Orleans, 96–100, 137

personal wealth, 6

personality, 55, 125

as Pony Express rider, 6, 17–21

and Pony Haslam, 96–97

popularity of, 3, 35, 68, 116, 124, 135

and Prentiss Ingraham, 39

promotes settling western US, 137

receives commission as colonel, 103, 105

receives Medal of Honor, 50

reenacting buffalo hunt, 21, *22*

returns to U.S., 108

and rise of mass media, 38

Scout's Rest Ranch, *84*

stage career, 28, 31–42, 43, 58

and television, 133, 135

and "The Star-Spangled Banner," 135, 137

treatment of American Indians, 125, 137

treatment of women, 78, 125, 137

wife, 116, 118

and Wild Bill Hickok, 35, 50

Wild West show (*See* Buffalo Bill's Wild West)

writes autobiography, 123

and Yellow Hair, 26–29, *27*

Cody, Louisa, 116, *117*, 118, 120, 139, 141

Cody, Wyoming, 137, 139, 141

Cody and Carver's Wild West, 45

Columbian Exposition, 112–116

combination. *See* Buffalo Bill's Combination

comic books, 58, 63, 65, 70, 130, 135

Cortés, Hernán, 8

"Cow-Boy Kid, The," 83

cowgirls, *114*

Crawford, Jack, 35, 36, 38, 47

Cunard Steamship Company, 89, *90*

Custer, George Armstrong, *4*, *27*, 34, 39

Deadwood Stagecoach, 45, 73, 97

Decker, May Cody, 123, 124, 137, 139

dime novels, 15, 17, 21, 39, 55–72

Dog Soldiers, 23–24

Edison, Thomas, 78, 133

Edward VII, King, 108

England, 74, 100, 103, 108

Europe, *101*, *109*, 111–112, 116, 124, *134*

faro, 92, 94–95, 98

Ferris, George Jr., 115

films. *See* movies
France, 111
Frizzle, John P., 89, 92

gambling, 94, 95
Golden Jubilee, 100, 103
"Golden West," 45, 49
graphic novels, 72

Haslam, "Pony" Bob, 96–97
Heygate, Reginald B., 89
Hickok, Wild Bill, 32, 35, 50
historical reenactments, *4, 6, 10,* 14, 21, 22, 24, 28, 73, *128, 129*
Hollywood. *See* movies
Holmes, H. H., 115
horsemanship, 73, 112, *114*

Indian Wars, 23–24, 26–28, 50
Indians. *See* American Indians
Ingraham, Prentiss, 17, 21, 39, 47, 58

Kansas Pacific Railroad, 6, 21, 41
"King of the Cowboys," 73

Life of Buffalo Bill (film), 130
Lillie, Gordon W., 122–123
Little Sure Shot. *See* Oakley, Annie
London, 100–102, 105–108
Lookout Mountain, 83, 139, 141

Majors, Alexander, 17, 21
Makharadze, Kishvardi, 77
Mardi Gras, 137
marksmanship, 76, 99
mass media, 38

McCoy, Tim, *13*
McLaughlin, James, 78–79
Merritt, Wesley, 26
Miller and Arlington's Wild West Show Company, 123–124
Mormons, 8
movies, 130–133, 135
Mudgett, Herman W., 115
murders, 115
Murphy, Audie, 38
music, popular, 137

National Football League, 130
Native Americans. *See* American Indians
Nelson, "Old Man" John Young, 73, 74
New Buffalo Bill Weekly, 68
New Orleans, 95, 96–100, 137
Newman, Paul, *132*, 135
nickel weeklies, *54,* 55–58, *56–57, 59, 61–62, 64, 66–67, 71*

Oakley, Annie, 6, *9,* 75, 76–78, 79, 96, 125
"Old Glory Blowout," 43, 52
Old West, 8, 43, 68, 131
Omonhundro, Texas Jack, 14, *33, 34,* 35, *36,* 41, 50, 99
"Original Wild West, The," 47

parades, 6, *104*
Pawnee, 23–24
Pawnee Bill, 122–123
Plains Indian Wars, 6
Pony Express, 6, 17–21, *20,* 96
popular culture, 131, 141–142
Powell, Frank, 98–99
promotional techniques, vii, 6, 8, 36

pulp magazines, 70

Red Right Hand; or, Buffalo Bill's First Scalp for Custer (play), 39
Red Shirt, Chief, 107
reenactment, historical. *See* historical reenactments
Roosevelt, Teddy, 135
Russell, William Hepburn, 17

Salsbury, Nate, 39–41, *40*, 43, 45
    as Buffalo Bill's Wild West manager, 47, 52, 76, 87, 95, 97, 100, 103, 111, 120
    death of, 122
Sandlot, The (film), 127, 130
scalp, *27*, 28
Scouts of the Prairie (play), 36, 60
Scouts of the Prairie, and Red Deviltry as It Is (Buntline), 34
Scout's Rest Ranch, *84*
Sells-Floto Circus, 123
serial killer, 115
sharpshooters, 6, 14, 43, 45, 76, 81, 83
Sheedy, Pat, 98
Sherman, William Tecumseh, 79
Sidney, Albert, 19
Sioux, 1, *10*, *25*, 26, 107
Sitting Bull, Chief, 78–81, *80*

"Star-Spangled Banner, The," 135, 137
State of Nebraska (ship), 105
Staten Island, 100
Street & Smith novels, 65, 68, 70
stunt shooting, 14
Summit Springs, Battle of, 24

Tall Bull, 23–24
Tammen, Harry, 123
Taylor, "Buck" William Levi, 73, 76
television, 133, 135
Turner, Frederick J., 115
Twain, Mark, 103
"Two Bills Show," 123

Victoria, Queen, 100, 103, 108

Waddell, William B., 17
Walks-Under- the- Ground, 77
West, American, vii, 8, 43, 47, 52, 68, 131, 137
Western Story Magazine, 68
Westerns, 133, 135
White City, 112
women, 76, 78, *114*, 125, 137
World's Columbian Exposition, 112–116

Yellow Hair, 26–29, *27*, 39

ABOUT THE AUTHOR

Kellen Cutsforth is the author of *Buffalo Bill, Boozers, Brothels, and Bare-Knuckle Brawlers: An Englishman's Journal of Adventure in America* (TwoDot, 2015) and *Buffalo Bill's Wild West Coloring Book*, and coauthor of *Old West Showdown: Two Authors Wrangle over the Truth about the Mythic Old West* (TwoDot, 2018). Since October 2018, Kellen has written a bimonthly column for the Western Writers of America (WWA) *Roundup* magazine titled "Techno-Savvy," where he discusses new technology for authors. He has published over thirty articles featured in such publications as *Wild West* and *True West* magazines. Kellen is also an active member of the WWA and is the social media manager for their Twitter account. He is a veteran speaker and presenter and has given multiple presentations for numerous history groups, libraries, and genealogical organizations. Kellen is also a past president of the Denver Posse of Westerners history group.